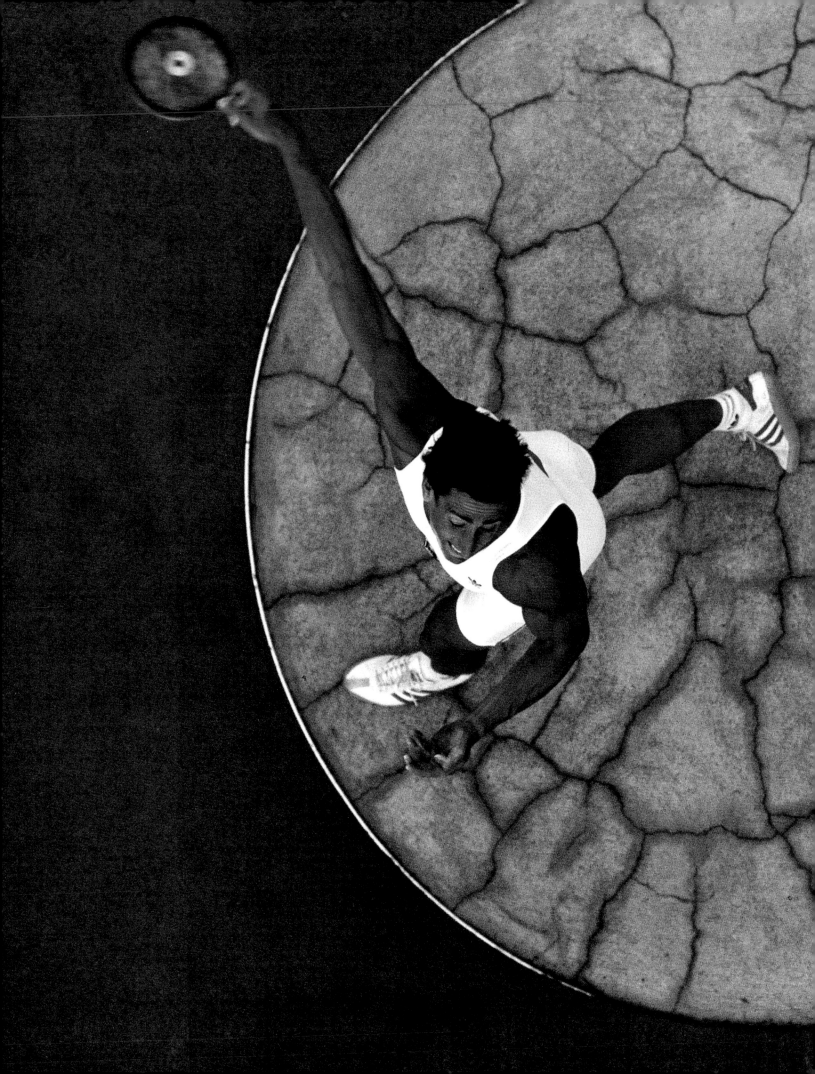

THE OLYMPICS

A HISTORY OF THE GAMES

Oxmoor House

BY WILLIAM OSCAR JOHNSON

© 1992, 1993
Time Inc.

SPORTS ILLUSTRATED is a
registered trademark of Time Inc.

ISBN: 0-8487-1115-7
Library of Congress Catalog Card Number:
91-067882

Manufactured in the United States of America
Second printing, 1993

Published by arrangement with
Oxmoor House, Inc.
Book Division of
Southern Progress Corporation
PO Box 2463 Birmingham, AL 35201

THE OLYMPICS
Project Director: MORIN BISHOP
  Copyreader: LESLIE BORNSTEIN
  Reporter: SALLY GUARD
  Photography Editors: TERESA CRAWFORD,
                EILEEN MILLER
Production Manager: ANDREW HUGHES
Designers: STEVEN HOFFMAN
        BARBARA CHILENSKAS

THE OLYMPICS was prepared by
Bishop Books, Inc.
611 Broadway
New York, New York 10012

Cover photograph (Eric Heiden, 1980):
Neil Leifer

To order SPORTS ILLUSTRATED magazine,
write to:
SPORTS ILLUSTRATED,
Subscription Service Department
P.O. Box 60001,
Tampa, Florida 33660–0001

CONTENTS

INTRODUCTION

NO ONE IS QUITE CERTAIN WHERE THEY CAME
FROM, AND GOD KNOWS NO ONE CAN GUESS
WHERE THEY ARE GOING, BUT AS WE SPEAK TODAY THE
OLYMPIC GAMES ARE ALIVE AND WELL AND LIVING OUT THE
LAST DECADE OF THE 20TH CENTURY AS ONE OF THE MOST SUCCESSFULLY
PACKAGED PRODUCTS OF OUR TIME. THAT'S SAYING A LOT SINCE JUST
ABOUT EVERYTHING IN OUR COMMERCIAL ERA SEEMS TO BE A PACKAGED

product—from professional wrestling to the U.S. presidency.

Of course, the Olympics weren't so easy to put in a package. They came in funny shapes, speaking many tongues, full of flags and bands and burning torches, awash in sweat, blood, tears and, in recent years, urine samples. In 1896, in their first modern reincarnation in Athens, they amounted to little more than a charming carnival of Boy Scoutish idealism. Immediately after that, they lurched into the 20th century like some sort of pestilence that infected every city it touched with an epidemic of bad temper and high-level confusion. In successive Olympiads they have been chameleonic, playing a series of radically differing roles depending on the spirit of their times. They have served as a surrogate battlefield for the cold war, a brightly lit stage in the world theater of protest, a slaughterhouse for bloodthirsty terrorists, a halfway house for blind idealists, an old-fashioned passion play pitting purest amateurs against foulest professionals, a glittering prime-time television sitcom. And much, much more....

In 1908 in London the Olympic Games inspired Irving Berlin to write, for the first time, both the lyrics and the melody of a song. The subject was Dorando Pietri, a courageous little Italian marathon runner who became the world's pet after he wobbled into the Olympic Stadium at the end of the race and staggered helplessly about until British officials helped him, all but comatose, across the finish line. Pietri was later disqualified, and Berlin's song probably should have been, too. It went, in part: *Dorando! Dorando! He run-a, run-a, run-a, run like anything./ One-a, two-a hundred times around da ring./ I cry, "Please a nun ga stop!"/ Just then, Dorando he's a drop!*

In 1936 in Berlin the Games served Adolf Hitler as a propaganda tool for his Third Reich, as everyone knows. Less well known is the fact that these Games also served as a functioning Nazi breeding farm to produce a crop of Olympic superbabies. Dr. Paul Martin, a highly respected Swiss surgeon and long-time Olympic runner who received an IOC diploma of merit in Berlin after competing in five consecutive Games, recalled this bizarre arrangement: "The Germans had reserved a sort of heavenly forest near the Olympic Village...[where] the prettiest handpicked maidens would offer themselves to the athletes—especially to the good Aryan types. Before submitting to the Olympic god of her choice, the girl would request her partner's Olympic badge. In case of pregnancy the girl would give this information to state or Red Cross maternities to prove the Olympic origin of her baby. Then the state would pay for the whole works."

In Tokyo in 1964 the Olympics served as a major catalyst—nay, catapult—to launch Japan on its way from an anemic and defeated nation to the fearsome economic giant it is today. Dr. Ryotaro Azuma, the mayor of Tokyo during those Games, recalled: "We were still struggling under a defeated enemy nation syndrome in the eyes of the world. Without the magic of the Olympic name we might not have gotten the investment we needed to rise as a world trade power. Our national prestige was tied to it."

Once upon a time the late Avery Brundage, the brassbound demagogue/idealist who was president of the IOC for 20 years, had the gall to say, "The Olympic movement is perhaps the greatest social force in the world. It is a revolt against 20th-century materialism. The Olympic movement appears as a ray of sunshine through clouds of racial animosity, religious bigotry and political chicanery. The Olympic movement is a 20th-century religion. Here there is no injustice of caste, of race, of family, of wealth...."

Brundage probably believed all this blather. But, in fact, under his arthritic rule, the so-called Olympic movement came to exist mainly for two purposes: 1) to congratulate itself and 2) to propagate itself. To those ends it produced a massive outpouring of hype, humbug and hypocrisy about amateur purity, political neutrality, racial equality, commercial pristinity—et cetera, et cetera. Most of that has been left out of the contemporary Olympic package. In its place we have cold business pragmatism. Money comes first. Salesmanship reigns. Merchandising rules. Olympic movement today means one thing—what else?—movement of the product. And in modern-day marketing the package produces the payoff.

This package, of course, is tied with strings that reach back into the mists of time. The Olympic Games may have begun around 1370 B.C. in small, simple, county-fair-sized events held on a grassy plain near the temple of Zeus in Olympia, and they may well have been an outgrowth of the rites of a cult of the dead. The evidence is imprecise. Not until 776 B.C. do we find verifiable evidence of a true Olympic Game—in the preservation of the champion's name. There was only one winner because there was only one event then, a footrace the length of the stadium, about 186 yards. Such simplicity could not long endure. Soon more events were added, including footraces of heavily armed men and the four-horsed chariot race, among others.

Everything that happened at the Olympics was ritually prescribed. The wild olive wreaths for the champions had to be cut with a golden knife by a child "still possessing both father and mother," from the sacred olive tree that was supposedly planted by Hercules himself near the temple of Zeus. When the crowns were awarded, a herald—who wore a victor's olive wreath for having won the Olympic competition for heralds—shouted the name of the victor, the name of his father and the name of his country, nothing more. The wreath itself was all the winner received at the Games. Of course, everyone knew well that there was more booty to come. Once the hero got home he was routinely given money and property. Streets were named for him, and the likes of Pindar or Euripides would sometimes toss off the odd ode in his honor.

But there was another side to ancient Olympic ritual that was not simply a matter of sport and its rewards. These Games were, in fact, wanton, bloody affairs. Ceremonies routinely included human sacrifices and oaths taken on pigs' entrails. One learned chronicler of these gruesome practices was Spiridion P. Lambros, a Greek scholar from the University of Athens, who cowrote the official history published by the Central Olympic Committee in Athens in 1896. Lambros painted a vivid portrait of excited multitudes strolling among colored tents through vendors' stalls and art exhibits spread over the grassy grounds near the Altis, or sacred grove of Zeus. "And yet," wrote Lambros, "this crowd, which awaited impatiently the celebration of the Games, and which contemplated the masterpieces at Olympia, could never mistake the character of the festival as they saw the smoke of the sacrifices rise and

heard the cries of the victims destined to be immolated on the altars of the Altis."

Blood was spilled everywhere—including all over many sporting events. Olympic boxing was a peculiarly violent sport in which competitors wrapped their fists and wrists with hardened leather thongs, sometimes gnarled with knots and knobs, sometimes studded with nails and metal balls. Various forms of disfigurement were so common that busts of boxers excavated from the ruins of Olympia showed mutilated

The pancration: perhaps the most brutal of the ancient Olympic events.

ears and missing noses as marks of honor. One winning boxer, Eurydamas of Cyrene, became a wildly acclaimed hero after the public learned that his opponent had broken many of his teeth, but that Eurydamas had quietly swallowed them to keep the man from realizing the damage he had done. An admirer of one Olympic boxing champion named Stratophon told the athlete, "After 20 years Ulysses was recognized from his appearance returning to his home, by his dog Argos. But thou, Stratophon, after boxing for four hours hast been so altered that neither dogs, nor any person in the town could possibly recognize thee. And if thou lookest at thy face in a mirror, thou thyself wilt swear that thou art not Stratophon."

The pancration, an event in which two men battled

until one quit, was even more brutal than boxing. No foul act or stranglehold was forbidden, no matter how violent, and the mayhem often included eye-gouging and the purposeful breaking of bones. The struggle went on until one man raised his hand from the ground to signal defeat.

There is a famous story of how a dead man became the winner of one such brutal battle. As chronicled by Lambros: "The Olympionikes, [Olympic champion] Arrachion, contending at Olympia for another crown, was so closely pressed by his antagonist, who had seized him round the body with his legs, while he squeezed his throat with his hands, that Arrachion to free himself was driven to break one of his toes. His opponent forced by the greatness of the pain extended his hand, as a sign of acknowledging himself defeated, but at that moment Arrachion expired, strangled by the pressure of his rival on his throat. None the less the crown was placed upon the corpse of Arrachion."

Ugly stuff. Difficult for the best of packagers.

The ancient Games hit quite another kind of nadir in 66 A.D. during the Roman occupation of Greece, when the villain emperor Nero insisted on competing while accompanied by 5,000 bodyguards. As the historian Lambros wrote: "All Greece, terrified, yielded to the ambitious emperor's desire for success.... everywhere the spectators applauded him, his rivals let themselves be overcome ... and the umpires hastened to lay at his feet crowns of which his head was not worthy." In the much beloved sport of chariot racing, Nero fell out of his vehicle, but the other racers pulled up, waited until he got back in and let him win the event in a walk. Lambros wrote mournfully, "The appearance of Nero in the Games shows clearly both what had been the decline of the Greek spirit, and how miserably the Olympic Games had fallen."

The Games struggled along under the Romans for another 300 years or so, until 393 A.D., when the emperor Theodosius abolished them. In the ensuing centuries, earthquakes, grave robbers and barbarian Goths did their dirty work around Olympia, and the hallowed place disintegrated. The Games were not seen again for 1,500 years.

The new Olympics, as we have seen, have risen to serve a myriad of non-sporting causes. But for the men and women who actually competed in these Games— the runners and jumpers, the winners and losers,

world-class athletes of every imaginable size and shape—the Olympics became special far beyond mere competition. Roger Bannister, the British miler who never won an Olympic medal but won immortality when he broke the four-minute-mile barrier in 1954, once said, "Records are ephemeral. The winning of an Olympic title is eternal."

This seemed overblown, very un-British, very un-Bannister. Yet athletes who went to the Olympics often returned to the real world with mystical interpretations of the experience. Bill Toomey won the decathlon at the 1968 Olympic Games in Mexico City at the relatively ripe age of 29 and afterward reported, "It's like being Peter Pan. It's like a window on your soul and you don't feel you will ever die."

Jules Ladoumègue, a Frenchman who won a silver medal at Amsterdam in 1928, said, "It was like something that seems to rise from the ground and carries you high into the sky. It is as if you were just born, and you can do nothing but remain very still, very happy. I have seen many things in my life, many things in the war, and I have cried many times in my life. But when the runner carries the flame into the stadium and the birds are freed and all the flags of the world are flying, I cry. I must cry."

Emil Zátopek, the fabled Czechoslovakian runner who won one gold and one silver medal in 1948 at the first post–World War II Games, recalled: "The revival of the Olympics was as if the sun had come out. The Olympics are the one true time."

Mustafa Dagistanli, a Turkish wrestler who won gold medals in 1956 and 1960, said, "Participants of countries still at the door of the Stone Age come to the Olympic Games. They compete, they win, they get beat, they return to their homes in the Stone Age. The Olympics is so beautiful, so big-hearted, so open to everything on the earth!"

So, however bizarre or hypocritical or overblown or laughable these Games may sometimes appear to us— neutral observers and nonparticipants on the sidelines—they do seem to reward those who compete in them with something wondrous beyond all other forms of sport. Beyond all other forms of life, for that matter. And perhaps that, by itself, is enough to justify the whole expensive, messy, magnificent creation as it has been delivered to us through the millenia. On the other hand, perhaps not. Please read on.

1896-1912

THE GAMES ARE REBORN

IN THE WINTER OF 1896, GEORGE STUART ROBERT-
SON, A BRILLIANT THOUGH WHIMSICAL STUDENT
AT OXFORD, READ ABOUT THE UPCOMING REBIRTH OF THE
OLYMPIC GAMES IN ATHENS ON A SMALL SIGN POSTED IN THE
WINDOW OF A LONDON TRAVEL AGENCY. "THE GREEK CLASSICS WERE MY
PROPER FIELD AT OXFORD, SO I COULD HARDLY RESIST A GO AT THE
OLYMPICS, COULD I?" SAID ROBERTSON YEARS LATER AS HE RECOUNTED

DE COUBERTIN, THE MAN WHO STARTED IT ALL,
SAW HIS FRAGILE CREATION HIT SOME EARLY POTHOLES BEFORE
REACHING SMOOTH PAVEMENT IN THE LATER YEARS

his vivid memories of those historic first Games.

By boat and train he traveled to Greece in time for the opening of the new Games on March 25. Robertson was a hammer thrower at Oxford, but this event was not included in the newborn Olympics, so he decided to enter the shot put and the discus throw. During his two-week Olympic odyssey, he spent a total of $11, finished fourth and sixth, respectively, in his two events and met the king of Greece to boot. "Nice chap," he recalled. "Sense of humor. Poor fellow. Assassinated at Salonika, wasn't he?" He was also introduced to Baron Pierre de Coubertin, the wealthy Frenchman who had originated the idea of a creating a modern Olympics. Robertson found him to be unimpressive and a bit puzzling. "Funny little man, the baron," he said. Actually, the baron was a deadly serious little man on a deadly serious mission to reform the world through his reinvented Olympic Games.

In Athens, he predicted that the new modern Olympics would eventually become both symbol and centerpiece of a new global era of togetherness among nations. "Men have begun to lead less isolated existences," he pontificated, "different races have learnt to know, to understand each other better, and by comparing their powers and achievements in the fields of art, industry and science, a noble rivalry has sprung up amongst them." The baron declared that the impact of new techonologies such as railway transportation and the telegraph, plus "an awakening taste for athletics everywhere" could not help but bring nations of this modern era together in celebration of this great sports spectacle. "The revival of the Olympic Games," he predicted, "will bring Athletism to a high state of perfection, and...will infuse new elements of ambition in the lives of the rising generation: a love for concord and a respect for life!"

This was perhaps too great a burden for the infant event to bear. Nevertheless, the Athens Games were well organized and proceeded with a minimum of the pompous military-religious ritual that enwrapped them in later decades. "There wasn't any prancing about with banners and nonsense like that," recalled Robertson. "I suppose we had some kind of Olympic fire. I don't remember it if we did." A total of 311 athletes from 13 countries turned up. The American team dominated track and field, the Germans gymnastics and the French cycling. The Greeks fared well, winning more medals than any other nation, but only one event really mattered to them: the marathon.

At 2 p.m. on the day of the race, 17 competitors—13 of them Greek—lined up on a bridge in the town of Marathon. At the sound of the gun, a speedy Frenchman leaped into the lead and set a suicidally fast pace: After just 32 minutes he was a full three kilometers (1.8 miles) ahead of the pack. Behind him were an Australian, an Englishman, a Hungarian and three Greeks—including Spiridon Louis, a professional water carrier from the town of Amarousion who had trained while he worked, jogging twice a day beside his water-bearing mule the nine miles back and forth between his village and Athens. The too eager Frenchman collapsed after the 32nd kilometer and was hauled away in an ambulance. Louis moved into the lead. King George, the royal family and thousands of excited Greek spectators waited anxiously in the stadium for word of the likely winner. Rumors raced through the crowd. At one point the Australian was reported to be winning. Hearts fell, spirits flagged. But then the police commissioner of Athens arrived on horseback and delivered the marvelous message to king and crowd: Spiridon Louis was the sure victor, and he was on his way to the stadium!

The water carrier arrived, sunburned and covered with dust, running flat-footed on dead legs toward the king. The stadium erupted in noise. Two princes left their seats and jogged alongside Louis toward the royal box. As the runner approached, the king stood and waved his yachting cap back and forth; the crowd waved tiny Greek flags in unison.

Later, when Louis left the stadium, grateful countrymen fought to give him whatever they had of value, littering his path with gold watches, watch chains and silver cigar cases. A tailor offered to make him suits for the rest of his life, a barber promised him free shaves forever, a restaurateur said he could always eat for nothing at his place. Louis said no to all of it because he wanted to preserve his amateur status. When King George asked him if he had a special wish, Louis said with a sigh, "Yes, please, a cart and a horse so I won't have to run after my mule anymore."

After the idyllic affair in Athens, there was every reason to expect that de Coubertin's creation would be a continuing quadrennial joy. But the baron had not figured on the pettiness and inefficiency of local athletic organizations. In Paris in 1900, after months of political infighting, the Olympics were shoehorned in as a sideshow to the five-month-long International Exposition. The word "Olympic" appeared nowhere in the official program, the only reference to the Games being the announcement of the *"Championnats Internationaux"* for *"Athlétiques Amateurs."*

At the outset the French had seemed determined to be friendly and efficient. Each competitor had been given a cozy sort of questionnaire that asked, among other things: "Were you reared as an infant naturally or artificially? What is the color of your beard? How strong was your grandfather?" What the French planned to do with such information remains unclear. But that minor mystery was quickly overshadowed by a series of surly confrontations between the French and their Olympic guests. Puritanical Americans were irked because the French scheduled events on the Sabbath. Amos Alonzo Stagg, who brought part of his University of Chicago track team to Paris, snapped, "It is a contemptible trick! Not a single American university would have sent a team had it not been definitely announced that the Games would not be held on a Sunday!"

Hahn: a triple sprint winner at the troubled 1904 Games.

Equally irksome were the conditions under which the athletes were forced to compete. Runners from all over the world were sore because the French refused to install a cinder track at Pré Catalan, the beloved city park, choosing instead to sketch a 500-meter oval on the undulating grass. And then there was the marathon, which, in contrast to the harmonious affair in Athens, was one of the more unsavory events in Olympic history. The race was run on a difficult and circuitous route through twisting city streets. As fate would have it, the winner was a Parisian baker's delivery boy, Michel Théato, who knew the route—as well as endless shortcuts—like the back of his hand. An American runner, Arthur Newton, recalled passing Théato halfway through the race, then not seeing him again until the finish, where Newton was shocked to discover Théato and another French runner, both of whom had been there for almost an hour. Adding to his suspicions was the state of the two runners' uniforms, immaculate in spite of the mud and water on the course. Nonetheless, the French victory stood.

After Paris, the modern Olympics badly needed a positive showcase to restore their reputation. Alas, the third Olympiad, in St. Louis in 1904, was even worse. It, too, was relegated to minor league status, held in the shadow of the World's Fair in celebration of the 100th anniversary of the Louisiana Purchase. Not surprisingly, the lion's share of the medals went to Americans, most notably Archie Hahn, who came away with golds in the 60-, 100- and 200-meter dashes. As in Paris, there was a marathon snafu, this one involving a phony winner who rode in a car part of the way. But St. Louis set an alltime Olympic record in bad taste with Anthropology Days, a sporting competition among "uncivilized tribes" including Pygmies, Moros, Sioux, Ainu and Patagonians, who competed against each other in such events as pole climbing, mud fighting and a tug-of-war. In the end, the official history of the World's Fair put Anthropology Days down as the only disappointing event of the summer because "representatives of the savage and uncivilized tribes proved themselves inferior athletes, greatly overrated."

De Coubertin did not witness the St. Louis fiasco, but when asked his opinion of it all, he responded with a very stiff upper lip: "In no place but America would one have dared to place such events on a program, but to Americans everything is permissible, their youthful exuberance calling certainly for the indulgence of the ancient Greek ancestors." With two horrid Olympiads on the record, the Greeks held an unofficial affair in 1906, in part to appease the Greek partisans who felt that the Olympics should always be held in their homeland. These were called the Intercalated (Interim) Games and were a smooth, happy operation from start to finish. In retrospect, they may have saved the Olympics for the rest of the 20th century, because the 1908 Games were as fouled by ill will as any to date.

This fourth Olympiad was to have been held in Rome,

but Mount Vesuvius erupted in 1906 and the Games were moved to London, where there were eruptions of quite another kind. The British hosts enraged the Americans in a number of ways: 1) by not flying Old Glory along with the other flags in the stadium, 2) by competing on the Sabbath and 3) by carrying the exhausted Italian, Dorando Pietri, across the marathon finish line to keep him from losing to the American, Johnny Hayes, who ultimately was ruled the winner.

Yet another British-American clash erupted over the 400-meter run. Newspapers around the land were foaming at the mouth before the finals, convinced that the three Americans in the four-man field were going to gang up on poor Wyndham Halswelle, the lone Englishman in the race, and try to bully him off the track. The British judges were warned in no uncertain terms not to let this happen. Sure enough, in the last 100 meters of the race, Halswelle tried to pass one of the Americans, John Carpenter, who ran wide to prevent him from taking the lead. British officials along the track began shouting "Foul!" prompting one overexcited British judge to jump onto the track and grab one of Carpenter's American colleagues in mid-stride. Yet another judge scurried to the finish and broke the tape before any Americans could get there and claim victory.

Then everyone deliberated about what to do next. After much discussion, the British-controlled jury disqualified Carpenter for impeding Halswelle and ordered that the race be rerun with just three contestants. Infuriated, the remaining two Americans refused to race again. Lieutenant Halswelle covered the 400 meters alone in a brisk trot and was duly awarded a sharply devalued gold medal for his trouble.

Ironically, all the bickering made the London Games front-page news all over the world, the first such widespread attention the Olympics had ever received. It also produced some amazing attendance figures. The tainted marathon, which ran from Windsor Castle to the royal box in the Olympic stadium in London, attracted 250,000 spectators along the course—the

Halswelle: the winner of devalued gold in the 1908 400 meters.

largest crowd ever recorded for a single sports event.

Then came the 1912 Games, a typically Swedish affair—clean and carefully choreographed—which attracted the most athletes to date (2,547) from the most countries to date (28). One hero was Jim Thorpe, the legendary Native American, who won gold medals in both the pentathlon and the decathlon. A supernaturally talented athlete and soaring free spirit, he was the toast of the town—happily drinking to himself and to anyone else game for some carousing. The other superstar in Stockholm was Hannes Kolehmainen, the first of the many distance-running Flying Finns who would grace the Olympics over the next couple of decades. He won gold medals in the 5,000 meters, 10,000 meters, marathon and 12,000-meter cross-country race. In his 3,000-meter leg of a team race he set a world record, although his team didn't win.

Another multiple gold medalist was Ralph Craig, an American who won the 200- and 100-meter dashes—the latter being infamous for its seven false starts. Craig recalled, "Yes, seven false starts. And I made one of them. Another American who had competed in the Paris Games—those 1900 Games were kind of horrendous, you know—he told me, if you ever get to the Olympics, if anyone moves a muscle, you go too. Don Lippincott [another U.S. sprinter] and I ran the whole hundred meters on one false start. The foreign officials were totally incompetent.... They did fire the recall gun, but I didn't believe it. At the end of the event—after all the false starts had finally stopped—they put up the flags. I looked up, and the one on the highest pole was for me. They gave the medals at the end of the Games. The king of Sweden gave us the gold medals. I went up twice, and he said to me, 'What, you again?' He was giving us wreaths, too. He didn't do his homework, he put the wreaths on wrong. The second time I went up, he got the wreath on right."

As it happened, in this Olympiad, the fifth time out, the modern Olympic Games were beginning to get it right, too. Finally.

THE EARLY YEARS

1 8 9 6 - 1 9 1 2

DESPITE THE BEST EFFORTS OF FOUNDER PIERRE DE COUBERTIN,

MANY OF THE EARLY OLYMPIADS WERE POORLY ORGANIZED, INEPTLY RUN AND

SPARSELY ATTENDED. NONETHELESS, THERE WERE ATHLETES WHO

PERSEVERED, HEROES WHO ENDURED AND PERFORMANCES THAT SET

THE STANDARDS FOR THE GENERATIONS TO COME

EARLY U.S. OLYMPIANS INCLUDED FRED WINTERS, WHO
FINISHED SECOND IN THE ALL-AROUND DUMBBELL
CONTEST IN 1904, AND THOMAS CURTIS (RIGHT), WINNER
OF THE 110-METER HURDLES AT THE 1896 GAMES

PARIS
1900

BENCHMARKS

1896
William McKinley
is elected
president.

1901
McKinley is
assassinated. Vice-
president Theodore
Roosevelt is sworn
in as president.

1902
Scott Joplin's
ragtime jazz is
wildly popular.

1903
Orville and Wilbur
Wright take the
first flight at Kitty
Hawk, N.C.

1906
The San Francisco
earthquake kills
thousands.

1909
Commander
Robert E. Peary of
the U.S. Navy
plants the
American flag at
the North Pole.

1912
An iceberg sinks
the Titanic off
Newfoundland,
drowning 1,595.

THE GAMES WERE A MERE SIDESHOW TO THE
INTERNATIONAL EXPOSITION IN PARIS (LEFT), BUT THAT
DIDN'T FAZE OLYMPIC LEGENDS SUCH AS JOHN FLANAGAN,
WHOSE GOLD MEDAL IN THE HAMMER THROW WAS THE
FIRST OF THREE HE WOULD WIN IN THE OLYMPICS

1904 SAW THE
INTRODUCTION OF DIVING
AS AN OLYMPIC SPORT;
RALPH ROSE (RIGHT)
TIED FOR FIRST IN THE
DISCUS BUT LOST TO
MARTIN SHERIDAN IN A
THROW-OFF; THE
AMAZING RAY EWRY (FAR
RIGHT) WON ONE OF HIS
10 CAREER GOLD
MEDALS IN THE STANDING
HIGH JUMP

THE GARTERS MAY LOOK ODD, BUT THEY DIDN'T KEEP MARTIN SHERIDAN FROM WINNING DISCUS GOLD IN 1904, '06 AND HERE IN '08; LITTLE-KNOWN REGGIE WALKER OF SOUTH AFRICA BECAME A LOCAL HERO AFTER HIS VICTORY IN THE 100-METER DASH (LEFT), WHILE DORANDO PIETRI MIGHT HAVE BEEN SO HONORED HAD HE NOT BEEN DISQUALIFIED FOR THE ASSISTANCE HE RECEIVED AT THE FINISH OF THE MARATHON (RIGHT)

S T O C K H O L M **1912**

TWO GIANTS MARCHED
WITH THE MERE
MORTALS AT OPENING
CEREMONIES (RIGHT):
HANNES KOLEHMAINEN,
FOUR-TIME GOLD MEDALIST
AND FIRST OF THE FLYING
FINNS, AND JIM THORPE
(ABOVE), THE MULTI-
TALENTED WINNER OF
THE DECATHLON AND
PENTATHLON WHO LOST HIS
MEDALS IN DISGRACE SIX
MONTHS LATER

HE WAS SMALL, BARELY FIVE feet three inches tall, and he cultivated a sweeping cowcatcher of a mustache beneath a nose that seemed made for a bigger man. Writing was his favorite pastime, pedantic, unpoetic stuff dealing with politics, history, education. He participated in sport very little, confining his activities to riding or rowing. In his late 20's, he came upon the theme that was to define his life: the "physical degeneracy" of France and the need to promote fitness and athleticism as a central tool "in the work of moral education." Eventually he tied all this together with the idea of resurrecting the long-dead Olympic Games.

He chose a November night in 1892 to spring his idea on the intelligentsia of Paris with a speech at the Sorbonne. He spoke of his hopes for "the diminution of the chances of war" and declared that the "cause of peace would receive a new and forceful boost" if nations competed on the athletic field rather than on the battlefield. He built to a crescendo, then proclaimed his central point that peace could be advanced through "this grandiose and beneficent work: *the re-establishment of the Olympic Games!*" The audience had no idea what he was talking about, and soon the baron was being peppered with questions.

"Do you mean a theatrical reproduction with fake athletes?" *Mais, non,* he said, the real thing.

"Then will the athletes be nude? Will women be forbidden to watch? Who will participate? Only the French?" It should be done on a world scale, he said.

They were laughing openly now. "Oh, then we'll have Negroes and Chinese and ... and ... redskins?" shouted one man. Disgusted, the baron left the podium.

But he was tough, and he had good connections. He convened an international meeting in Paris in 1894 with leading sportsmen from nine countries, and after a week of wining, dining and entertaining them, he engineered a unanimous vote to exhume the ancient Olympic Games in Athens in March 1896. When the Greek government balked at the expense, de Coubertin got the king of Greece and his sons to lead a fund-raising campaign. They convinced George Averoff, a wealthy Greek philanthropist, to donate the million drachma ($184,000) for a new stadium.

At the opening ceremonies, the statue unveiled at the stadium entrance was not that of the French aristocrat who had created the Games, but of Averoff, who had merely paid for them. Ultimately the baron would receive the credit he deserved, but definitely not in Athens. He kept saying "I hereby assert once more my claims for being sole author of the whole project." However, when he returned home, his wife confronted him with the cruel question, "Why was it that not one time did they mention your name at any ceremonies?"

The hideous Games in Paris in 1900 were not the baron's fault. He had been shunted aside by officious organizers until the last minute, when it was too late to salvage the situation. The Paris Games of 1924, which he oversaw as president of the International Olympic Committee, were far more successful, and when they were over, he resigned with the satisfaction of a job well done.

In the final years of his life, he lived in Lausanne and was occasionally seen rowing alone on Lake Geneva. His ancient family fortune was gone, and he lived with his shrewish wife and mentally disturbed daughter in a hotel suite provided free by the city of Lausanne.

He was nominated for the Nobel Peace Prize in 1936 and was deeply disappointed when the jury did not select him. He had hoped that the prize might serve as validation of his lifelong belief in the Games as a vehicle for world peace. "He was very disillusioned, very sad, at the end of his life," said his nephew, Geoffrey de Navacelle.

The baron died of a stroke on Sept. 2, 1937, at the age of 74. In his will he decreed that he should be buried in Lausanne but that his heart should be removed from his body, encased in a marble column and shipped off to be buried at Olympia in Greece. His wish was granted.

OLYMPIC RESUME: *Pierre de Coubertin, the father of the modern Olympics, served as president of the International Olympic Committee from 1896 until his retirement in 1924.*

FOR A MAN WHO SPENT THE bulk of his years in the mundane role of hydraulics engineer for the New York City Water Department, Ray Ewry managed to accumulate a list of pretty otherworldly accomplishments. Consider the following:

No Olympian in history has won as many gold medals as Ewry did. His total was 10.

No Olympic track and field athlete has ever gathered so much gold at such a relatively advanced age. Ewry won his first three

golds in Paris in 1900 at the not-so-young age of 26. His last two came in London in 1908, by which time he was a virtual codger of 34.

Outside track and field there are several relatively easy-for-geezer Olympic events, such as fencing, sailing, dressage, etc., in which older athletes can reasonably expect to fare well against younger competitors. But Ewry won all 10 of his golds in standing jumps—events that were launched from a dead-still, feet-flat-on-the-ground start. No run-up, no momentum, no power-trigger at all save the pure coiled muscle of his legs. A world-record standing jump was the sort of feat you would expect from a well-conditioned young gazelle not a loyal waterworks employee in his 30's.

Adding further to the Ewry legend was his traumatic childhood. Born in 1873 in Lafayette, Indiana, Ewry was devastated by polio as a young child and confined to bed and a wheelchair until doctors decided that he should try to develop his muscles through exercise. He took up calisthenics and eventually added jumping to his daily routine.

By the time he enrolled at Purdue in 1890, Ewry had grown to 6' 3" and had acquired the nickname "Deac," perhaps in deference to his deep religious convictions. He stayed for seven years, earning both undergraduate and graduate degrees in mechanical engineering and serving as captain of the track team.

After finishing at Purdue, he moved to New York and began his career in hydraulics. He joined the New York Athletic Club, and, as a member of that prestigious group, he took part in the folly-filled 1900 Games in Paris. There

he found himself competing under absurdly poor conditions. The bad-tempered French had refused to provide the jumpers with a patch of hard ground from which to take off because they didn't want to destroy so much as a blade of grass in Pré Catalan. Instead, Ewry was forced to launch his airborne forays from a heavily watered grass surface, an experience not unlike bouncing in a bog.

None of this fazed Ewry. In fact, on a single historic day, July 16, 1900, he won three gold medals in a matter of hours. First he sprang over the bar in the standing high jump at a record 5' 5"—only 7¾" below the running high jump mark that won the gold medal in Paris. Next, from another swampy takeoff, he produced a standing long jump of 10' 6¼". Finally he made yet another soggy takeoff for a standing triple jump of 34' 8½". One day, three events, three gold medals—a starburst of Olympic victories that has never been matched since.

In St. Louis in 1904 he won three golds again. After that, the standing triple jump was eliminated from Olympic competition, leaving Ewry with only two events, both of which he won at the so-called Intercalated (or Interim) Games in Athens in 1906 as well as at the 1908 Games in London. Ewry's record was perfect: He had entered 10 events and won 10 gold medals. He had never even finished second.

As time for the Stockholm Olympics drew near, Ewry was training hard, fully expecting to make it 12 for 12 in '12. But he soon realized that he had lost a bit of spring and, at 38, he retired as the undefeated Olympic champion of standing jumpers. After 1912, his two other events were eliminated. Thus, properly, his records will stand forever.

OLYMPIC RESUME: *Ray Ewry's total of 10 individual gold medals in the standing long jump, standing triple jump and standing high jump is the highest in Olympic history, three more than his nearest competitor, gymnast Vera Cáslavská of Czechoslovakia.*

AFTER JIM THORPE WON BOTH the pentathlon and the decathlon at the 1912 Olympics in Stockholm, King Gustav of Sweden handed him, among other prizes, a bust of the king himself and a silver chalice in the shape of a Viking ship, which was lined with gold, embedded with jewels and weighed 30 pounds. The chalice was a gift from the czar of Russia. As Thorpe lugged the loot back to his place in the ranks of the American team, he muttered, "What the hell do I do with this?" Ultimately he had no choice: A year later both the bust and the chalice were taken from him and shipped back to IOC headquarters in Lausanne, Switzerland. There the chalice sat for many dusty years on a museum shelf—symbol of what happened to a naive young Native American caught in the clutches of the self-righteous puritans who ran "amateur" athletics in those days.

The story is well known: Six months after his double triumph in Stockholm, a Massachusetts newspaper reported that Thorpe had been paid (perhaps as little as $2 a game, it was later revealed) in the summers of 1909 and 1910 for playing semipro baseball in North Carolina. When the Amateur Athletic Union asked him about the charges, he pleaded guilty in a letter that was heartbreaking in its innocence: "I did not play for the money...but because I liked to play ball. I was not wise in the ways of the world and did not realize this was wrong, and that it would make me a professional in track sports...I am very sorry...to have it all spoiled in this way and I hope the Amateur Athletic Union and the people will not be too hard in judging me." The judgment was about as hard as it could possibly be. The AAU tendered to the Olympic authorities its "apology for having entered Thorpe and having permitted him to compete at the Olympic Games of 1912," and concluded with the icy declaration: "The AAU will immediately eliminate his records from the books."

Thorpe's gold medals were then awarded to the two second-place finishers, one a Norwegian, the other a Swede. Both kept the medals all their lives, although they frequently declared their willingness to return them to Thorpe should the decision be reversed.

As decades passed, Thorpe became an increasingly sympathetic, not to say pathetic, figure. In 1950 the Associated Press declared him the greatest male athlete of the first half of the 20th century, but by then he had become a bloated caricature of himself. In March 1953, he died an alcoholic in a trailer park in Lomita, California.

A campaign was begun to restore his amateur status and his Olympic victories, but there was powerful resistance in both the AAU and the Olympic movement, none greater than that put up by a bespectacled Chicagoan named Avery Brundage, who had lost to Thorpe in Stockholm. Known as "Old Ironsides" for his dogged approach to training, Brundage had been considered America's main hope in the pentathlon, but he finished a dreary sixth behind the dazzling Thorpe. In the decathlon he was 15th.

For decades, sports historians wondered whether Brundage, as president of the USOC and later of the IOC, was exacting revenge for those early defeats in his refusal to consider reinstatement of Thorpe's victories. In an interview with Robert W. Wheeler, author of a book about Thorpe, Brundage was typically pitiless.

Wheeler: Why do you resist all efforts to restore Thorpe's medals?

Brundage: You don't know much about the law, do you, kid?

Wheeler: What do you mean?

Brundage: Ignorance is no excuse.

Not until 1982 did the IOC finally approve Thorpe's reinstatement, and even then it chose to dilute his victories by listing him as "co-winner" of both events. Old Ironsides had been dead for several years, but no doubt would have approved this last attempt to diminish the great American hero.

OLYMPIC RESUME: *Jim Thorpe became the only man to win both the decathlon and the pentathlon with his double victory at the Stockholm Games in 1912. His fame continued in later years, most notably through his role as one of pro football's pioneering players.*

ALVIN KRAENZLEIN

AS A STUDENT AT THE UNI-versity of Pennsylvania, Alvin Kraenzlein was an idol to track buffs well before his heroics at the star-crossed Paris Olympics. At one time or another during 1900, he held six world records, and he was widely celebrated as the man who had revolution-ized hurdling by introducing the more graceful style used today—extending one leg ahead over the hurdles instead of jumping over with both legs tucked up as most competitors did then.

In Paris, Kraenzlein was stylish in much more than clearing hurdles. Throughout the Games, when he wasn't competing, he strolled about dressed to the nines, wearing a saucy cloth cap, an Eton collar and a smart cravat. Indeed, the American team in general got high marks for haberdashery in Paris. An admiring observer wrote, "The natty college costumes of the Americans were a decided contrast to the homemade attire of some of the best European athletes." But if Kraenzlein & Co. looked well put together in their public appearances, in private the 55-man U.S. team was a bick-ering gang of backbiters drawn from various college teams and the New York Athletic Club. A major sticking point among them was whether or not to compete on Sun-day, a practice that was universally taboo back in the puritanical environs of the 46 States.

Ultimately each college or club team decided separately on the matter. Penn allowed its athletes to choose individ-ually, leading several of them to say to hell with the Lord's day—including Kraenzlein, who wanted to compete in the Sunday final of the long jump. Some of the other teams opted to honor the Sabbath. This might not have mat-tered—except that it meant the man who held the world record in the long jump, Meyer Prinstein of Syracuse, could not compete in the final. Nonetheless, his jump of 23' 6¼" recorded during the trials would be carried over to Sunday, and if no one surpassed it, he would get the gold medal. Unfortunately, Prinstein had assumed that Kraenzlein, his closest rival, would not jump on Sunday.

But Kraenzlein did jump, launching a leap that crept past Prinstein's mark by a single centimeter. This narrow defeat made Prinstein so angry that he challenged Kraenzlein to a jump-off on Monday. When the Penn man refused, the Syracuse man punched him, and their nattily dressed teammates had to drag them apart.

Bad tempers and bad management were, of course, the hallmark of the 1900 Games. Baron de Cou-bertin himself said after-ward, "We made a hash of our work." As it turned out, Kraenzlein's other three gold medals—in the 110-and 200-meter hurdles plus the 60-meter dash—were won on a surface that vaguely resembled hash: Thanks to the French refusal to install a real track at Pré Catalan, Kraenzlein and his rivals were forced to compete on soft and uneven grassy turf. In 1898, on a proper track, he had set a world record of 23.6 seconds in the 200-meter hurdles. In Paris, his time over hash was 25.4.

Kraenzlein was in dental school at Pennsylvania when he produced his Olympic triumphs. After he won his last gold medal, he declared, "That was my last race. I am through with athletics and shall devote myself to some-thing more serious." He did neither. He never practiced dentistry, and eventually he became a vagabond track coach who would go anywhere as long as the pay was good. In 1913 he went to Germany for a reported $50,000 to prepare German track and field athletes (who had never won a gold medal to that point) for their upcoming national showcase: the Berlin Olympics of 1916. World War I canceled those Games and, presum-ably, Kraenzlein's contract. After that he coached at Michigan for a time; then he went to Cuba in 1924 to prepare its team for the second Paris Olympics. For the record, Alvin Kraenzlein himself won as many gold medals in 1900 as Cuba did in all of its Olympic appear-ances through 1972.

OLYMPIC RESUME: *Alvin Kraenzlein was the first man to win four individual gold medals at a single Summer Games, with vic-tories in the 60-meter dash, the long jump, the 110-meter hurdles and the 200-meter hurdles.*

1920-1936

THE GAMES GROW UP

THOUGH THE ANCIENT GREEKS DID SOMETIMES

POSTPONE WARS SO THE OLYMPICS COULD TAKE

PLACE, NO ONE WAS SO NAIVE IN THE 20TH CENTURY AS TO

EVEN BRING UP THE IDEA. BETWEEN 1914 AND 1918, WORLD WAR I

SPREAD ITS CARNAGE ACROSS EUROPE, AND THE NEXT APPOINTED

OLYMPIC YEAR—1916—GLIDED PAST ON A RIVER OF BLOOD. THE SUPREME

IRONY WAS THAT THE IOC HAD OFFICIALLY SELCTED BERLIN AS THE

SONJA HENIE, THE DARLING OF THREE
CONSECUTIVE OLYMPIC GAMES, SET THE STANDARD FOR THE
FIGURE SKATING DIVAS TO COME

host city for the 1916 Games. The same hierarchy that might have produced a sleek and disciplined Olympic show was instead launching mankind's first massive poison gas attacks and instigating some of the gruesomest battlefield slaughters in the history of war.

The world had not recovered from nor forgiven the horror by the summer of 1920, when the Olympics began in Antwerp, and the Games were a bizarre and mournful affair. As usual, the American team traveled to Europe by ship—and what a ship it was. "The government gave us this great rusty old army transport," recalled Dan Ferris, secretary-treasurer of the Amateur Athletic Union. "When we arrived to board, they had just taken off the bodies of 1,800 war dead from Europe. The caskets were sitting there on the docks, lines and lines of coffins. The smell of formaldehyde was dreadful. The place was infested with rats.... It was a shocking way to start."

With only a year to prepare for the Games, Antwerp was hardly in a state of readiness. Recalled Alice Lord Landon, a U.S. diver with the first contingent of American women to compete in an Olympics: "Poor Antwerp wasn't really ready for something like the Olympics. We had cornhusk mattresses, and the women lived in a YWCA hostess house while the boys were in a horrible school barracks. The swimming and diving competition was held in part of the old moat that used to surround the city in ancient times. It was the clammiest, darkest place, and the water was frigid.... It looked bottomless and black, and from the high board it looked like you were diving into a hole all the way to the center of the earth. It terrified me, and I did terribly."

By 1924 the world's wounds were healed, and an international festival of sport was in harmony with the times—enough so that there were not one, but two Olympics that year. The first Winter Games were held in January in the lovely Alpine village of Chamonix, France, beneath the glowering visage of Mont Blanc. It was a tiny, fun affair with just 294 athletes from 16 countries and an opening day parade that included the local fire department, mountain guides and the village council along with the athletes. The very first Winter Olympic gold medal went to an American boy from Lake Placid, New York, Charlie Jewtraw, who won the 500-meter speed skating race. Jewtraw recalled, "I stood in the middle of the rink, and they played *The*

Star-Spangled Banner. The whole American team rushed out on the ice. They hugged me like I was a beautiful girl. My teammates threw me in the air ... oh, my god ... it was like a fairy tale."

The idea of a Winter Olympics had been resisted by the International Olympic Committee and Baron de Coubertin for fear that a winter celebration would create a spirit of disunity within the Olympic movement. Well, it hasn't—and it certainly did not in 1924. Originally the IOC had scheduled the Summer Olympiad for Amsterdam, but when the baron decided it was time for him to resign the presidency of the IOC, the committee chose to honor him by making Paris the host city for his valedictory Games. It was a memorable affair, drawing a record 3,092 athletes from 44 countries. The glowering Finnish running genius, Paavo Nurmi, won five gold medals, and the handsome American swimming hero, Johnny Weissmuller, won three. There were a few nasty episodes—hyperfanatic French sports fans booed during the playing of other nations' anthems, and a French spectator caned an American art student for "loud rooting" during a U.S.-France rugby match. But all in all Paris was credited with producing the best Olympiad so far, and the baron stepped down gracefully, saying, "My work is done." He meant what he said, for he never appeared at another Olympics, although six more were held, Winter and Summer, before he died.

By quitting in 1924, the baron missed being entangled in the revolutionary and controversial changes that occurred as his idealized Olympics evolved into more complex, more worldly spectacles. Amsterdam hosted the 1928 Summer Games and provided the first hint of the specialized corporate-style management that would come to typify Olympic teams of the future. The U.S. track team had a manager, three assistant managers, a head coach, 10 assistant coaches, a trainer and five assistant trainers. The men's team won exactly one individual gold medal. As it turned out, medals were spread among more nations than ever before—including 10 golds for the former outlaws from Germany, who were allowed to compete for the first time since the war.

In 1932 the Olympics, both Winter and Summer, visited the U.S. for the first time since the distasteful fiasco in St. Louis in '04. The Winter Games were held in the nondescript upstate New York village of Lake

Placid. The world was caught in an economic depression, and only 306 athletes from 17 countries competed. Scandinavians won the bulk of the skiing medals, to no one's surprise, while Americans dominated speed skating. One Yank who earned extra ink was Eddie Eagan, a young lawyer who held degrees from Yale, Harvard and Oxford. As a member of the U.S.'s winning four-man bobsled team, Eagan received a gold medal in Lake Placid. He had also won a gold medal in 1920 in Antwerp as the light heavyweight boxing champion, making him the first person to win gold medals in both the Summer and Winter Games. No one knew at the time what a rare eagle this Eagan was to be: He is still to this day—60 years and 27 Olympiads later—the only athlete who has achieved that feat.

After cold, dull Lake Placid, Los Angeles was Eden. Day after sunny day, records were routinely shattered as stars like Babe Didrikson and Buster Crabbe grabbed the spotlight. Some experts predicted—though wrongly—that many of these new world marks would never be improved upon because of the "freak California climate" in which they were set. Everything about the L.A. Games was wildly successful. One million people paid $2 million to attend, and many more would have been there were it not for the Depression and the distant Pacific

Didrikson and Rogers: two of the stars at the glitzy '32 Games.

location. The California approach to the Olympics was typically exuberant—and money-oriented. Zack Farmer, a former cowboy and L.A. real estate baron who was chairman of the local organizing committee, coolly described the Games afterward: "The '32 Games were the first ones that ever paid off.... We gave them a wonderful Olympics and a profit to boot. Hell, it's all just a business proposition."

The most original—and most controversial—element in the L.A. business proposition was the Olympic Village. It covered 250 acres and housed male athletes from all 37 countries. There had never been anything like it. Farmer recalled, "You have no idea the resistance to it at first. These different

countries were afraid of political and racial differences. They all squawked they had training secrets and didn't want to live close together.... [But] that village was the marvel of the Games. We damn near had to drive the athletes out to get them to go home after the Games. It was the most grand and pathetic thing you ever saw, those big hulks practically cried. They *loved* it." When the Games were over, the flimsy portable bungalows in which the athletes had lived were dismantled and sold to tourist courts and construction companies. Farmer bragged, "We salvaged everything for 100 cents on the dollar!"

Besides bringing big business to the Olympics, Los Angeles also introduced show business to the festivities. Celebrities such as Will Rogers, Joe E. Brown, Gary Cooper and Clark Gable were in the crowd at competitions. Mary Pickford and her husband, Douglas Fairbanks Sr., entertained favored Olympians at their famed mansion, Pickfair. One of their regular guests was Takeichi Nishi, a lieutenant in the Japanese cavalry who won a gold medal in Los Angeles in the Prix des Nations equestrian event. Born a baron and socially very polished, Nishi had a wife in Tokyo whom he rarely saw. He once sent her a postcard from Los Angeles that said, "I'm being very popular here. Bye-bye." Nishi's ties to America continued to be very strong long after the Olympics, and his wife recalled that the great horseman was despondent when his country attacked Pearl Harbor in 1941. But, loyal soldier that he was, he went to war, and in 1945 died in an island cave during the great American invasion of Iwo Jima.

Japan's presence at the Los Angeles Olympics was also made noteworthy by its swimmers—a team of unknown teenagers who stunned the world with a remarkable string of victories. There was deep suspicion among their opponents that such success could only have been the result of some kind of Oriental trickery. Crabbe, who won a gold medal in L.A. and went on to become Hollywood's seventh Tarzan, recalled, "A well-known American coach was convinced the Japanese were doped. They were winning everything, and when they got out of the pool, they'd have these bright red marks on their faces. This made him so suspicious. Do you know what it was? They'd been sniffing oxygen, and the marks were from their oxygen masks—legal as hell."

If Los Angeles brought movie stars and the profit motive to the Games, Berlin introduced the more sinister concept of the Olympics as ideological battlefield and athletes as political ammunition. As Richard Mandell wrote in *The Nazi Olympics:* "A trend that was strengthened by the results of the 1936 Olympics was to view athletes increasingly as national assets procurable like fighter planes, submarines, or synthetic-rubber factories.... After 1936 a stable of athletes became necessary for national standing."

The IOC awarded the '36 Games—Winter and Summer—to Germany in 1931, before Hitler came to power. When he became chancellor in 1933, many people assumed that he would cancel the Olympics. For one thing, Nazi youth and anti-Semitic groups had labeled the Games "an infamous festival dominated by the Jews." For another, Germans had done poorly in Los Angeles, winning only four gold medals—including one for a poem in the widely ignored cultural competi-

The Nazi Games: Hitler's chance to strut his stuff on the world stage.

tion. But Hitler saw the propaganda value of the Games and plunged ahead. With 755 athletes from 28 nations, the Winter Games at Garmisch-Partenkirchen were a modest success, and the führer could boast of his nation's six medals out of the 51 awarded. But it was the Summer Games in Berlin that he saw as his real opportunity to strut his stuff on the world stage.

And strut he did. In fact, the Third Reich spent an unprecedented $30 million on the Summer Games, building a 100,000-seat stadium, six gymnasiums and a swimming stadium, plus state-of-the-art electronic timing devices, photofinish equipment and radical new press facilities—including the first telex and a zeppelin to transport newsreel film out of Germany. The Nazis

also built an Olympic Village of handsome brick-and-stucco cottages that made L.A.'s tacky bungalows look like privies. To make certain no one missed their point, they placed one of the L.A. shanties on display.

Berlin was flooded with military uniforms during the Games, and roars of "*Sieg Heil!*" thundered out of every Olympic audience. The militarism was chilling, but even worse was the blatant Nazi anti-Semitism. Sentiment in the U.S. was painfully divided over whether to compete, but the powers on the United States Olympic Committee were determined to send a team. President Avery Brundage released an official statement saying "the persecution of minority peoples is as old as history" and "the customs of other nations are not our business." General Charles H. Sherrill, a member of both the USOC and the IOC, said, "It does not concern me one bit the way the Jews in Germany are being treated, any more than lynchings in the South of our own country."

Of course, the U.S. did compete, along with 48 other nations, the most to date. The sterling performances of American blacks—especially Jesse Owens with his four gold medals—did much to undercut the white supremacy credos of the Nazis. Nevertheless, U.S. officials played out their own ugly anti-Semitic role to the end. There were six American sprinters prepared to run on the four-man 400-meter relay team. Two of them, Marty Glickman and Sam Stoller, were Jews—the only Jews on the U.S. track team. Not only did they not run in the relay, but they were also the *only* two members of the team who did not compete in any events in Berlin.

There was much evil in the air in Berlin. Soon there would be another war and yet more blood that would wash away the Games of 1940 and 1944. The IOC in its supreme political wisdom had chosen Japan as the host nation for '40 and was forced to cancel due to Japan's brutal invasion of China. World politics were obviously not the strong suit of these Olympic Colonel Blimps. And after 1936 the Games would be held hostage to politics for many years to come.

1920

ANTWERP

WITH THE WAR OVER, THE OLYMPICS

WERE RESTORED, BUT THE WORLD WAS STILL IN MOURNING, AND

THE GAMES PROVED TO BE A POORLY ORGANIZED AFFAIR. IT WOULD TAKE

TIME—AND STARS LIKE PAAVO NURMI—TO RETURN THE

GOLDEN GAMES TO THEIR FORMER LUSTER

THE AMAZING NURMI BEGAN HIS LONG-DISTANCE
DOMINANCE WITH THREE GOLD MEDALS; SPECTATORS
ENJOYED THEIR SURROUNDINGS (RIGHT) DURING
THE PLATFORM DIVING COMPETITION

ANTWERP
1920

JACK KELLY'S GOLD MEDAL
IN THE SINGLE SCULLS
COMPETITION CONFIRMED
HIS STATUS AS THE WORLD'S
FINEST OARSMAN. YEARS
LATER HIS DAUGHTER
GRACE WOULD CHARM
THE NATION AND
PUT THE KELLY NAME
BACK IN THE NEWS

ANTWERP **1920**

A RECORD 29 NATIONS
GATHERED TO WATCH
STARS LIKE CHARLEY
PADDOCK (RIGHT, WINNING
THE 100-METER DASH) AS
WELL AS NEWCOMERS LIKE 14-
YEAR-OLD GOLD-MEDALIST
AILEEN RIGGIN (ABOVE
RIGHT, NEAREST U.S. FLAG)
AND FELLOW DIVERS NILS
SKOGLUND AND HELEN
WAINWRIGHT

BENCHMARKS

JANUARY
Booze is banned as Prohibition becomes the law of the land.

APRIL
The new fashions are out, hemlines are up, and the long, lithe look is in.

AUGUST
After an 81-year struggle, women win the right to vote.

SEPTEMBER
The Black Sox scandal rocks the world of baseball as eight members of the Chicago White Sox are accused of fixing the 1919 World Series.

DECEMBER
The British House of Lords approves the division of Ireland into two parts, and the "troubles" enter a new phase.

1924

PARIS
CHAMONIX

THESE WERE THE UNFORGETTABLE GAMES OF *CHARIOTS OF FIRE* —

THE LAST TO BE ORCHESTRATED BY FOUNDER PIERRE DE COUBERTIN

BUT THE FIRST TO INCLUDE THOSE STRANGE

AND CAPTIVATING EVENTS ON SNOW AND ICE THAT CAME TO BE

KNOWN AS THE WINTER GAMES

ROBERT LEGENDRE DIDN'T MAKE THE U.S. LONG JUMP TEAM
BUT SET A LONG JUMP WORLD RECORD IN THE PENTATHLON;
JOHNNY WEISSMULLER (RIGHT) TOWERED OVER THE GAMES,
WITH A COMBINED FIVE GOLDS IN '24 AND '28

44

CHAMONIX 1924

BENCHMARKS

JANUARY
Lenin dies at the
age of 54.

FEBRUARY
George Gershwin's
*Rhapsody in
Blue* is performed
for the
first time.

FEBRUARY
King Tut's coffin,
sealed for
3,300 years, is
opened in Luxor,
Egypt.

APRIL
Metro Pictures,
Goldwyn Pictures
and the Louis B.
Mayer Company
join forces to form
MGM.

JUNE
Franz Kafka
dies at
the age of 40.

SEPTEMBER
Ten-year-old
Jackie Coogan
meets the
pope and declares
Rome "the best
place in the world
for shooting
pictures, after
Hollywood."

AMONG THE FIRST GOLD MEDALISTS IN THE
HISTORY OF THE WINTER GAMES WERE CHARLIE JEWTRAW,
THE FIRST OF ALL THE WINTER WINNERS, IN
THE 500-METER SPEED SKATING RACE (ABOVE LEFT);
HERMA PLANK-SZABO IN THE WOMEN'S
FIGURE SKATING COMPETITION (LEFT); AND JACOB
TULLIN THAMS IN THE 90-METER SKI JUMP

AMSTERDAM **1928**

BENCHMARKS

JANUARY
Thomas Hardy
dies at
the age of 87.

JUNE
Amelia Earhart
becomes the first
woman to fly across
the Atlantic.

AUGUST
Joseph Schenk, the
president of United
Artists, claims that
talkies will never
catch on.

AUGUST
The U.S., France,
Great Britain,
Germany and 11
other nations sign
the Kellog-Briand
Treaty outlawing
war.

OCTOBER
Dr. Mansfield
Robinson claims to
have received a
message from Mars
over his wireless,
but he needs time
to decode it.

NOVEMBER
Herbert Hoover
is elected
president in a
landslide.

WITH A COMBINED
THREE GOLD MEDALS IN '28
AND '32, AMERICA'S
IRVING JAFFEE WAS A
NOTABLE EXCEPTION TO
THE SCANDINAVIAN
DOMINATION
OF OLYMPIC SPEED
SKATING EVENTS

1932

LOS ANGELES
LAKE PLACID

EVEN THE GREAT DEPRESSION COULDN'T DAMPEN THE SPIRITS AT

THESE ALL-AMERICAN GAMES, PARTICULARLY AT THE STAR-STUDDED SUMMER

VERSION IN LOS ANGELES, WHERE ATHLETES AND SCREEN

IDOLS EXCHANGED ADMIRING GLANCES AND WORLD RECORDS FELL IN

ASTONISHING NUMBERS

BUSTER CRABBE'S GOLD MEDAL LED TO SCREEN ROLES AS
TARZAN, BUCK ROGERS AND FLASH GORDON; JEAN SHILEY
(RIGHT) THRILLED HER U.S. TEAMMATES BY BEATING THE
BOASTFUL BABE DIDRIKSON IN THE HIGH JUMP

LOS ANGELES 1932

DIDRIKSON BACKED UP HER BRAG WITH GOLD
MEDALS IN THE JAVELIN THROW AND THE 80-METER
HURDLES IN ADDITION TO A SILVER IN THE HIGH
JUMP; ATHLETES SUCH AS GOLD-MEDALIST ATTILIO PAVESI
OF ITALY (LEFT) MUST HAVE ENJOYED THE
SCENIC PACIFIC COASTLINE AS WELL AS THE LOVELY
L.A. BEACHES (BELOW)

LAKE PLACID
1932

BENCHMARKS

JANUARY
At the age of 90, Oliver Wendell Holmes resigns from the Supreme Court.

FEBRUARY
Construction begins on Rockefeller Center in New York City.

MARCH
The 20-month-old son of Charles Lindbergh is kidnapped from his home in New Jersey.

JULY
Flo Ziegfeld dies of pneumonia at the age of 63.

AUGUST
Eleven million Americans are still out of work.

NOVEMBER
FDR defeats Herbert Hoover in the presidential election. The electoral total is 472–59.

THE 10,000-METER
SPEED SKATING RACE DREW
A CROWD (ABOVE);
ANDREE AND PIERRE
BRUNET (LEFT) WON THE
PAIRS FIGURE SKATING
COMPETITION IN BOTH '28
AND '32; THE GOLD-MEDAL
WINNING U.S. BOBSLED
TEAM (FAR LEFT) INCLUDED
EDDIE EAGAN (SECOND
FROM LEFT), THE ONLY MAN
TO EARN GOLDS AT BOTH
THE WINTER AND
SUMMER GAMES. THE
CONDITIONS WERE SO POOR
THAT THE FOUR-MAN
BOBSLED EVENT
WAS HELD AFTER CLOSING
CEREMONIES

1936

BERLIN
GARMISCH-
PARTENKIRCHEN

THE IMAGES ARE CHILLING: SWASTIKAS ON ARMS, A NAZI

SALUTE, THE BLOOD-RED FLAG OF THE THIRD REICH. THESE WERE THE GAMES

OF ADOLF HITLER, HIS CHANCE TO SPREAD THE UGLY RELIGION

OF RACIAL HATRED—BUT THEY WERE ALSO THE GAMES OF A SHARECROPPER'S

SON NAMED JESSE OWENS, WHO TOLD A DIFFERENT TALE

WHILE HITLER POSTURED FOR THE CAMERAS, OWENS WENT
TO WORK ON THE TRACK, DESTROYING THE MYTH OF ARYAN
SUPERIORITY WITH FOUR GOLD MEDALS—AND WITH THE
QUIET DIGNITY OF A GENUINE HERO

BERLIN
1936

THE 1,500-METER
RUN FEATURED SIX OF THE
TOP SEVEN FINISHERS FROM
'32 AND WAS WON IN
WORLD-RECORD TIME BY
NEW ZEALAND'S
JACK LOVELOCK (LEFT),
WHO SPRINTED AWAY FROM
THE FIELD WITH AN
UNUSUALLY LONG
FINISHING KICK. LOVELOCK
LATER SETTLED IN THE
U.S. AS A PHYSICIAN IN
NEW YORK CITY. SUFFERING
FROM DIZZY SPELLS
AS A RESULT OF A FALL
FROM A HORSE, HE WAS
KILLED IN 1940, WHEN HE
FELL IN FRONT OF A
SUBWAY TRAIN

GARMISCH
1936

BENCHMARKS

MARCH
Hitler violates
two treaties
and invades the
Rhineland.

MAY
Italy conquers
Ethiopia, and
Mussolini declares
that "Italy at last
has her empire."

JUNE
Lucky Luciano is
found guilty of
"compulsory
prostitution."

JULY
Francisco Franco
and his
fascist troops
begin the Spanish
civil war.

NOVEMBER
FDR is reelected
in a landslide
over Alf Landon
with the largest
voter turnout in
U.S. history.

DECEMBER
Edward VIII
abdicates the
British throne to
marry American
divorcée Wallis
Simpson.

OLYMPIC AND NAZI SYMBOLS WERE
SHAMELESSLY INTERMINGLED AT THE SKI JUMPING
COMPETITION (LEFT); THE INCOMPARABLE
SONJA HENIE CAPTURED HER THIRD CONSECUTIVE GOLD
MEDAL IN THE FIGURE SKATING COMPETITION

AFTER A NINE-YEAR CAREER as a swimmer, Johnny Weissmuller could boast, "I never lost a race. Not even in the YMCA. The closest I ever came to losing was on the last lap of the 400-meters in 1924 when I got a snootful. But I knew enough not to cough and I won." That coughless win brought him a gold medal in the Olympic Games in Paris, where he won two more for swimming plus a bronze for playing on the American water polo team. In the 1928 Games in Amsterdam he won two

more golds for swimming. Over his full career Weissmuller set no fewer than 51 world records from 50 to 800 meters—an incredible span of distances that is the track equivalent of the 100-yard dash to the 5,000-meter run.

He had fully expected to remain unbeaten through the Games of 1932, but good fortune intervened. "I was training for the Los Angeles Olympics," he recalled, "when I was offered a five-year, $500-a-week contract with BVD swimming suits. Big Bill Bachrach, my coach, said, 'Sign, John.' I signed. From then on, I'd go around to swimming shows and get paid to tell people, 'You swim faster in our suits because the stripes go up and down.'"

And that was just the beginning. "One day I was in L.A., and they asked me to do a screen test for Tarzan. I ran around in a little bitty loincloth, I climbed a tree, I picked up this girl and carried her around. There were 150 Tarzans trying out. I went back to selling BVD suits. Then I got a wire: COME BACK. YOU'RE TARZAN…. That's how fast your life changes."

Weissmuller was accustomed to abrupt changes before that. He grew up poor, raised mainly by his mother, who was a cook at a German sports club in Chicago. At 15 he came under the enormous wing of Bachrach, the coach of the Illinois Athletic Club, who weighed at least 300 pounds. "He was like a father to me," Weissmuller recalled, "[but]…with Bachrach, you better darn well be a champion. He once kicked me in the stomach to make a point. Once in Hollywood when I was doing Tarzan, we wondered if an elephant could swim in deep water. We pushed in a little elephant—1,000 pounds or so—and he

swam just like a dog. The director decided I ought to swim with the elephant, and I did. The elephant gave me a hell of a kick in the rib cage, and I darned near sank to the bottom. That kick reminded me of Bachrach."

But the behemoth and the boy swimmer made a great team—not unlike a pair of accomplished confidence men. "When we would go to meets we were supposed to get eight dollars, nine dollars a day [expenses] from the AAU," Weissmuller recalled. "Bachrach'd tell a meet promoter, 'Listen, I'll get Johnny to break a record for you. It'll get lotsa publicity for your pool. Then you give me $100.' They'd wonder if that wouldn't make me a pro, but Bachrach'd say, 'No, you're giving the $100 to me. I'm the pro, not Johnny.' With the $100 we'd eat steaks instead of mush and sleep in hotel suites instead of cots in a dormitory."

Unfortunately, once Weissmuller signed on as Tarzan, his partnership with Bachrach dissolved. Weissmuller did 12 Tarzan movies, a season of Jungle Jim episodes on TV and earned several million dollars. However, he went through five wives and countless business partners over the years, and his fortune was dissipated in many ways. "My trouble," Weissmuller once said, "is that I believe everybody. I sign the paper where they tell me to sign."

In the early 1960s, he moved to Florida from California: "A friend of mine in Fort Lauderdale gave me a condominium free. I asked him why, and he said, 'I figure your name is going to help fill it up.' It happened. It filled up in two years, and he told me I had to move out."

Johnny Weissmuller died in January 1984 at the age of 79. He had been rendered an invalid by several strokes in 1977 and was broke and living in Acapulco with his fifth wife, Maria. He still had never lost a swimming race.

OLYMPIC RESUME: *Johnny Weissmuller won a total of five gold medals in the 1924 and 1928 Games, with two wins apiece in the 100-meter freestyle and the 800-meter freestyle relay as well as a single gold in '24 in the 400-meter freestyle.*

S O N J A   H E N I E

PRESS AGENTS AND HEAD-line writers labored to come up with sprightly new nick-names for her: The Norwegian Doll, Pavlova of the Silver Blades, the Nordic Golden Girl and, of course, the Nasturtium of the North. Damon Runyon called her "a gee-whizzer." TIME put her on the cover of its July 17, 1939, issue. The occasion was the release of her fourth film, *Second Fiddle*, in which she played Trudi Hovland, a skating schoolmarm from Bergen, Minn., who is called to Hollywood after a local swain sends her photograph to a studio. Trudi-Sonja encounters a press agent played by Tyrone Power, and after a mistaken-identity romance involving the crooner Rudy Vallee and some ice show production numbers, she winds up in Power's arms. Suffice to say, it was pretty awful, and TIME wrote of her career in films: "Sonja Henie's ambition is to do one without her skates. Judging from the acting Trudi Hovland does … with heavy dramatic lines like, 'Let me go, Aye tall yu,' this ambition will take some realizing."

But skating would remain her calling—as it had been for her entire life. When she was a roly-poly child of 11, she competed in the Olympics at Chamonix and finished eighth out of eight. Undeterred, her well-to-do father, Wilhelm, a wholesale fur merchant in Oslo, simply intensified his support and paid for the best teachers on earth—including the great Russian ballerina Tamara Karsavina. It was Henie's inclusion of ballet flourishes in her routines plus her revolutionary wardrobes—short skirts, ermine-trimmed satin costumes, white skate boots instead of black—that made her so exciting. She won 10 straight world championships, starting at age 14 in 1927, and collected three straight Olympic golds following her failure in Chamonix.

Her personal life was less successful. On July 4, 1940, she married Dan Topping, a millionaire New Yorker who later owned the Yankees. Trouble loomed early, for he was a jovial playboy and she was a health fanatic, always dieting and insisting on two massages every day plus some kind of strenuous daily exercise—skating, skiing, tennis,

swimming, even hockey. The two divorced in 1946. She married Winthrop Gardiner Jr., socialite-sportsman, in 1949, but that marriage lasted only seven years.

Despite the turkey-on-ice quality of most of her films, she once ranked third behind Shirley Temple and Clark Gable as a box office attraction and earned more than $200,000 a year—a fortune at the time. Her ice shows were consistent money-makers, and as the years passed she progressed from star to manager to owner, becoming a multi-millionaire in her own right. She faced serious financial trouble only once, after an opening night disaster in Baltimore in March 1952 when a section of bleachers collapsed and injured 277 spectators. The show was closed, and nearly $6 million in lawsuits were filed. Fourteen months later, a jury found Henie and her company blameless.

She returned to Norway in 1953 for the first time in 15 years and renewed her acquaintance with a rich Norwegian shipowner and art collector, Niels Onstad, whom she had known since she was a child. In 1956 they married and art became their shared passion. Over the years their collection came to include works by Renoir, Matisse, Picasso and Klee among many others.

The couple had homes in Los Angeles, Manhattan and Lausanne as well as in Oslo, where they spent four months a year at their estate, Grandholtet. The walls of the bar there were covered with memorabilia, including a photograph that showed Henie shaking hands with Hitler after her victory in the 1936 Games at Garmisch-Partenkirchen. Norwegians were bitter that she would display such a photo, given the Nazis' brutal occupation of Norway, but she kept the picture up anyway. Her marriage to Onstad was a lasting, happy one, and on Oct. 12, 1969, Sonja Henie died of leukemia in his arms aboard an ambulance plane carrying them from Paris to Oslo. She was 57.

OLYMPIC RESUME: *Beginning in 1928, Sonja Henie won three consecutive gold medals in figure skating, establishing herself as the first in a long line of glamorous women's figure skating champions.*

BABE DIDRIKSON

LOS ANGELES IN 1932 WAS A city that doted on its movie stars—their egos, their assignations, their opinions, their appetites. But even in the Hollywood sea of dross and glamour, Mildred (Babe) Didrikson stood out as something special. She was outrageous, boasting endlessly of her unlimited abilities. She once walked up to Helene Madison, who held 15 world swimming records, and asked her how fast she could swim the 100-meter freestyle. Madison told her, and Babe snorted, "Shucks, lady, I can beat that by three seconds just practicin'."
Headline writers dubbed her Whatta-Gal Didrikson, Texas Tornado, Terrific Tomboy. Sportswriters adored her, and Grantland Rice, the leading scribe of the day, declared that she was "the most flawless section of muscle harmony, of complete mental and physical coordination the world of sport has ever known," meaning that in his opinion she was not only the greatest woman athlete ever, but the greatest athlete of *either* sex.

By the time the 1932 Games began, Babe's loud mouth had made her many enemies, especially among her U.S. teammates. But she instantly proved that her bragging was more than empty talk: Her first try with the javelin flew 143' 4"—a toss that no competitor was able to match. In her next event, the 80-meter hurdles, she won again, this time setting a world record. However, an American colleague, Evelyne Hall, crossed the line in precisely the same time and had a welt on her neck that she insisted was caused by hitting the tape first. After a debate the judges gave the gold to Babe—not a popular decision among her teammates.

Her last event was the high jump, and her chief competitor was another American, Jean Shiley. They wound up tied at a world-record height of 5' 5¼". Both missed at the next height, so the judges set the bar back for a runoff. Shiley cleared it. Babe did, too—except this time the judges decided that she had dived headfirst over the bar, a technique that was illegal in those days. They gave Shiley the gold and Didrikson the silver. Later Shiley recalled, "Babe left the field very, very angry. The other girls on the team

were delighted, like children at Christmas, because I had beaten Babe. I was under terrible pressure, you know, because they had spent the last two days in my room saying, 'We couldn't beat her, Jean, *you've* just got to beat her, cut her down to size.'"

After the Games, Didrikson traveled the vaudeville circuit to cash in on her newfound fame. She appeared on stage in a Panama hat, a knee-length green coat and high-heeled Spectators. She sang a song, *I'm Fit As a Fiddle and Ready for Love*, then took off her heels, put on rubber-soled track shoes and removed her coat to reveal a red, white and blue jacket and satin shorts. A treadmill began turning in front of a black velvet backdrop with a large clock attached. Babe started running on the treadmill, faster and faster, as the clock showed her speed. At last, she burst through a finishing tape and took a bow. Then she hit a few plastic golf balls into the audience and wound up her act playing superb harmonica renditions of *Jackass Blues* and *Begin the Beguine*. She was called back for encores every time.

She also played baseball with the itinerant House of David team for a time, enduring a killing schedule of 200 games a year. She recalled, "I was an extra attraction to help draw crowds.... I had my own car.... I'd pitch the first inning, then take off and not see the team again until the next town."

Of course, all the while she was doing these odd and somewhat demeaning things, she was practicing to add yet another sport to her astonishing repertoire. Before she died of cancer in 1956 at the absurdly young age of 45, she had come to be arguably the best woman golfer in the world. She had also mellowed considerably. Patty Berg, a great golfer in Babe's day, recalled after her death: "Sometimes I find myself leaning back in a chair thinking about Babe, and I have to smile. She was the happiest girl you ever saw, like a kid."

OLYMPIC RESUME: *In 1932, Babe Didrikson won gold medals in the 80-meter hurdles and the high jump. She would later move on to golf, winning 12 major tournaments, including three U.S. Opens.*

ON AUG. 17, 1936, ONE DAY after the Berlin Olympics ended, a dispatch was filed from London by the International News Service under Jesse Owens's byline. It said, "I am turning professional because, first of all I'm busted and know the difficulties encountered by any member of my race in getting financial security. Secondly, because if I have money, I can help my race and perhaps become like Booker T. Washington." Initially Owens's four gold medals did produce some dazzling offers of big money.

A Harlem club owner said Owens could earn $10,000 for a one-night stand, and Eddie Cantor wired him to "hold tight" for a deal that promised $50,000 for a personal tour. The best offer of all came from a startling source: the Republican presidential campaign of Governor Alf Landon of Kansas who was running against President Franklin Delano Roosevelt.

Owens signed on and made some short speeches for Landon, who wound up winning exactly two states, Vermont and Maine. Owens recalled, "Poorest race I ever ran. But they paid me a *lot* — I won't say how much, but a *lot*. I was the guy who was the beginning of the celebrity stable in political campaigns, I guess."

Another kind of payoff came in December 1936, when Owens received $2,000 for defeating a horse in a footrace in Havana. "Of course, there's no way a man can *really* beat a horse, even over 100 yards," Owens said many years later. "The secret is, first, get a thoroughbred because they are the most nervous animals on earth. Then get the biggest gun you can and make sure the starter fires that big gun right by that nervous thoroughbred's ear. By the time the jockey gets the horse settled down, I could cover about 50 yards." He was criticized for stooping to such tawdry methods to cash in on his medals. He replied, "People said it was degrading for an Olympic champion to run against a horse, but what was I supposed to do? I had four gold medals, but you can't eat four gold medals. There was no television, no big advertising, no endorsements then. Not for a black man, anyway. Things were different then."

He had grown up in deep poverty. "My parents were not literate people — how could a sharecropper in Alabama in the first 20 years of this century get to be literate?… We picked cotton all day long. When I was seven, I was picking 100 pounds a day. The cotton stalks were taller than me, and I'd practically drown until the sun was high and the dew dried some. It was hard. After working like demons for the summer, there still wasn't enough money to last the winter."

Once the post-Olympic glow faded, he found himself scrambling again to survive. He traveled with a circus-basketball team called the Indianapolis Clowns. "We'd get into these little towns and tell 'em to get out the fastest guy in town and Jesse Owens'd spot him 10 yards and beat him." He fronted for an itinerant dance band: "They had me sing a little, but I couldn't carry a tune in a bucket. We went to garden spots like Monroe, Louisiana. There'd be knife fights right on the dance floor some nights…. It was a long way from the Olympic ideal."

Owens prospered nicely during the last four decades of his life largely by making dozens of inspirational speeches every year. He was once described as "a professional good example." He had a strong, deep voice and spoke in the operatic style of the great black preachers. His speeches were full of shibboleths and clichés, but the fact that they were spoken by the great Olympian Jesse Owens made them almost sacred. He once said, "Grown men stop me on the street and say, 'Mr. Owens, I heard you talk 15 years ago in Minneapolis. I'll never forget that speech.' And I think to myself, that man probably has children of his own now. And maybe, maybe he remembers a specific point I made. Maybe he is passing that point on to his own son just as I said it. And then I think — that's immortality! You are *immortal* if your ideas are being passed from a father to a son to his son and on and on and on…."

OLYMPIC RESUME: *Jesse Owens dominated the 1936 Games with gold medals in the 100- and 200-meter dashes, the 400-meter relay and the long jump. Not until Carl Lewis in 1984 would another man win as many golds in track and field at a single Games.*

WHEN PAAVO NURMI WAS only 26 years old, a statue of him was erected in a park in Helsinki. Two years before Nurmi died, in 1973 at the age of 76, a friend remarked, "Just think, Nurmi has had to look at his own statue for 48 years. What would that do to a man?"

In Nurmi's case it was clearly not an inspiration. As the most celebrated distance runner of the 20th century grew older, he seemed to grow ever more sour, ever more miserly, ever more reclusive. He certainly deserved to get more pleasure out of his career, because no one was ever greater at his events.

In all he entered 12 Olympic races from 1920 through 1928, winning nine gold medals and three silvers. Over his 10 best seasons, he broke or equaled every world record in every one of his distances, which included one mile, two miles, three miles, four miles, five miles, six miles, 1,500 meters, 2,000 meters, 3,000 meters, 5,000 meters, 10,000 meters and 20,000 meters. He also ran farther in one hour than anyone before him—11 miles 1,648 yards.

He was born in 1897 in bitter poverty in Turku, the former capital of Finland, 100 miles northwest of Helsinki. His father died when he was 12, forcing Nurmi to quit school and go to work as an errand runner, pushing a heavy wheelbarrow through the streets of the city. In his teens he began running alone through the surrounding black pine forests. Soon, excited by his newfound passion, he changed from a glum, unresponsive boy to a loquacious gabber who talked so much about running that people avoided him. An old friend said, "It was the replacement for his father. Running was Nurmi's attempt at finding real life."

He cashed in on his fame whenever he could. In 1925 he toured the U.S. and was profoundly offended to find himself gawked at as a circus freak whose secret of success was a constant diet of black bread and fish. At one point a reporter noted that Nurmi was scarfing a lunch of meat and rolls, and said, "What? No black bread and fish today?" To which Nurmi replied with a sneer, "No black bread and fish *any* day."

There were many questions and at least one investigation over the years about his "amateurism," but his name was always cleared—at least until 1932 when his variety of quasiprofessional activities resulted in his disqualification from the L.A. Games. This prevented him from trying for a gold medal in the only Olympic distance run he had never entered—the marathon. Finland went into national mourning over his demise, and Nurmi more or less became a hermit. Nevertheless, he managed his money so well from seclusion that he eventually built himself a fortune in real estate as well as a prosperous sporting goods shop.

In 1952 he made a surprise appearance at the opening ceremonies of the Olympic Games in Helsinki, carrying the Olympic torch on the final lap around the stadium track. At first the crowd was silent, for there had been no warning that Nurmi would be there. Then, slowly, the noise rose from a low rumble to a deafening roar. Even the dour Soviet team, competing in an Olympics for the first time since the Russian Revolution in 1917, broke ranks and rushed to the edge of the track to applaud as the Flying Finn ran by. Despite the storm of emotion raging around him, Nurmi himself remained stony, offering no smile and not the slightest gesture of gratitude.

Years later, in the 1960s, Nurmi suffered a massive coronary, and not long before his death he announced a sizable bequest to a foundation that supported heart research. In connection with the gift he agreed to hold a brief talk with reporters. One asked him, "When you ran Finland on to the map of the world, did you feel you were doing it to bring fame to a country unknown by others?"

"No. I ran for myself, never for Finland."

"Not even in the Olympics?"

"Above all, not then. At the Olympics, Paavo Nurmi mattered more than ever."

OLYMPIC RESUME: *Over three Olympiads, Paavo Nurmi won 12 medals, including nine golds—the most won by any man except for Ray Ewry. His five gold medals in 1924 are the most ever won in track and field at a single Games.*

ELEANOR HOLM FIRST COM-peted in the Olympic Games in 1928, a Brooklyn fire-man's daughter who, at 15, was "still at the age where it was a big kick to go out with my father and ring the bell on his shiny red car." She won no medals in her spe-cialty, the backstroke, in those Games, but in Los Angeles in 1932 she won a gold medal, and by the time the 1936 Olympics in Berlin rolled around, she had won 29 U.S. championships and held six world records. Nat-urally, when she boarded the SS *Manhattan* with the rest of the U.S. Olympic team for the nine-day crossing to Europe, she was a clear favorite to win again.

She was still only 23, but she had long grown out of childhood thrills. "I had been around. I was no baby," she recalled. "Hell, I married Art Jarrett after the '32 Games. He was the star at the Coconut Grove, and I went to work singing for his band. I used to take a mike and get up in front of the band in a white bathing suit and a white cowboy hat and high heels. I'd sing *I'm an Old Cowhand*. Warner Brothers had signed me as an actress—not a swimmer, an actress. Anyway, here I'd been working in *nightclubs* when I made the team in '36. Actually, I quit the band a month before the trials to go into training for the Olympics."

On the ship she spent a lot of time in the first-class sec-tion with sportswriter friends, although members of the team were supposed to stay in compartments below decks—"in *steerage*," as Holm described it, "four to a room, way down in the bottom of the boat where every-thing smelled like liniment!"

One night she had been carousing in first class with some newspapermen when, as she recalled it, "This chap-eron came up to me and told me it was time to go to *bed*. God, it was about nine o'clock, and who wanted to go down in that damn *basement* to sleep anyway? So I said to her, 'Oh, is it really bedtime? Did *you* make the Olympic team or did I?' I had had a few glasses of champagne. So she went to [USOC president Avery] Brundage and complained that I was setting a bad example for the team, and they got together and told me the next morn-ing that I was fired. I was heartbroken!"

Nevertheless, Eleanor Holm pulled herself together and became the belle of the Berlin Games, a favorite of everyone from the U.S. newspaper crowd to the Nazi hierarchy. "I was listed as a correspondent for INS or someone, but I never wrote a word," she recalled. "Paul Gallico wrote every-thing under my name. I was asked to all the Nazis' big receptions, and, of course, Brundage and all the big shots would be there too, trying to ignore me!… Göring was fun…. Lots of chuckling. And so did the little one with the clubfoot [Josef Goebbels]. Hitler asked to see me, and through his inter-preter he said if I'd been on the German team, they'd have kept me on the team and then punished me after the Olympics—if I had *lost!* Hitler asked me himself if I got drunk—he seemed very interested—and I said no."

When she got home after the Games, Holm's bandlead-er-husband considered suing the USOC and Brundage for damages. "But then we started getting all these fabu-lous offers and he dropped it," she said. "I did all right after I won in 1932, but 1936 made me a *star*, a goddamn glamour girl! Just another gold medal would never have done that!"

Her life after Berlin was tempestuous with a couple of broken marriages and lurid tabloid accounts of an alleged suicide attempt. She starred for a long time in the Aqua-cades, a showbiz amalgam of singing, dancing and swim-ming created by her second husband, Billy Rose. For the past 25 years she has lived relatively quietly in the Miami area. "Life owes me nothing," she said recently. "I've had a *ball!*"

OLYMPIC RESUME: *Known more for her exploits outside the pool than her performances inside it, Eleanor Holm was nonetheless one of the dominant swimmers of her era, with a gold medal in the 100-meter backstroke in 1932. She had not been defeated in seven years by the time the 1936 Games got under way, and she held six world records.*

1948-1960

THE GAMES EXPAND

THE GAMES RETURNED IN 1948 AFTER SKIPPING

TWO OLYMPIADS TO MAKE ROOM FOR YET

ANOTHER WAR OF HORRENDOUS COST. THE WINTER OLYMPICS

WERE HELD IN THE QUAINT RESORT OF ST. MORITZ IN BEAUTIFUL,

NEUTRAL SWITZERLAND, WHICH HAD NOT BEEN DAMAGED AT ALL IN THE

WAR. IN CONTRAST, THE MOOD FOR THE SUMMER GAMES IN LONDON WAS

DARK, ALMOST MOURNFUL. THE CITY HAD BEEN HEAVILY BOMBED, AND

AL OERTER WAS A GENUINE
GIANT OF THE OLYMPIC GAMES, WITH DISCUS
GOLD MEDALS IN 1956, '60, '64 AND '68

rubble-strewn ruins were still common. Food rationing continued. There was a housing shortage, and no money was available for a new stadium (old Wembley did the job) or for an Olympic Village (a sprawling ex-RAF barracks served). Japan, Germany and Italy, as former enemy nations, were barred from competing. The Soviet Union had not been to an Olympics since the Russian Revolution in 1917 and did not participate this time, either.

Missing also was one of the greatest track stars of all time, Gundar Hagg, the magnificent Swedish miler who had flirted for years with the magic four-minute mark (his best time was 4:00.2 in 1946). London would have been his first Olympic appearance, and he almost certainly would have won a gold medal in the 1,500-meter run. But, alas, Hagg had been disqualified for professionalism. He was philosophical about it: "The decision to disqualify was correct enough if you followed the regulations. In a good running season I could make 30,000 crowns ($6,000), which was paid under the table by promoters.... However, the penalty was arbitrary, and many lesser-known breakers of the same law went without punishment. In a certain way I'm thankful because the decision forced me to quit while I was on top."

The brightest star of the London Games was Fanny Blankers-Koen of the Netherlands, a mother of four who won four gold medals in sprints and hurdles. Almost as successful was Micheline Ostermeyer of France, a concert pianist who won gold medals in the discus and the shot put as well as a bronze in the high jump. The pianist did not get half the ink in the British press that "The Flying Housewife" did, but she was a far rarer bird. Her grandfather was the composer Lucien Laroche; a great-uncle was Victor Hugo. Ostermeyer practiced the piano five or six hours a day, a far cry from the paltry five or six hours a week— mostly at night—that she devoted to her sports. She had not expected to win, and she was exultant after she did: "The Olympics were the biggest moment of my life." Nevertheless, she found that her concert career was adversely affected by her sporting success. "If I had played tennis or something mundane like that, it might have been all right, but other musicians thought—*track and field?* There was prejudice. [For a long time] I could not play Liszt [because] he was too *sportif*. I had to play Debussy, Ravel, Chopin. Then in

1954 or 1955, I finally played Liszt at a recital, and I had such a success with it that I thought, Oh, *why* didn't I play it before?"

The subdued show in London was followed in 1952 by a hard-eyed Cold War confrontation in Helsinki, where the Soviets finally made their Olympic debut. Parry O'Brien, then 20 and about to win his first of two golds and a silver in the shot put over three Olympiads, recalled, "We had no idea what to expect. They might have been a population from another planet. For all we knew, the Russians had a guy who could throw the shot 80 feet and another who could high jump nine feet and another who could run the mile in three-and-a-half minutes. They were a total mystery to the world."

The Soviets did everything they could to maintain that mystique. They refused to live in the Olympic Village and made plans to airlift their competitors daily from Leningrad. Finding this scheme impractical, they then decided to erect their own village in Otaniemi, close to a Russian-owned naval base. They surrounded the premises with barbed wire and guards. All of this made them appear to be every inch the fearsome "Red Menace" that millions of Americans already believed them to be.

In the States, less than a month before the Games began, Avery Brundage had organized a 14½-hour Olympic Fund Telethon, starring Bing Crosby and Bob Hope, to raise $500,000 to finance the American Olympic effort. Hope set the tone: "I guess Old Joe Stalin thinks he is going to show up our soft capitalistic Americans. We've got to cut him down to size." Fifty million people watched the show, and, under the spell of pleas from Frank Sinatra, Abbott & Costello, Ginger Rogers, Dinah Shore, George Burns and Gracie Allen, the audience pledged $1 million. Alas, when the pledges were collected, there was only $353,000.

As it turned out, the shortfall didn't hurt the American cause in Helsinki. While the U.S. men racked up 14 gold medals in track and field, the Soviet men came away with none. Overall, the U.S. won 76 medals to the U.S.S.R.'s 71, and although it wasn't the blowout triumph over Communism that Bob Hope–style capitalists might have liked, it was quite acceptable.

The Soviets had skipped the 1952 Winter Games in Oslo, but in 1956 they showed up in force in the Italian village of Cortina d'Ampezzo and led all nations with 16 medals. This not only embarrassed the U.S. (seven medals) but also humiliated Norway (four), which had been the leading medal-winning nation in five of the previous six Winter Olympiads. Toni Sailer, Austria's skiing wunderkind, almost matched the Norwegian total all by himself, with gold medals in the three Alpine events.

That same year, as Americans back home engaged in hysterical cold war rhetoric, the Soviets at the Summer Games in Melbourne practiced their own paranoia. They had convinced themselves that Olympic venues were swarming with undercover Central Intelligence Agency operatives—all working night and day to corrupt Soviet athletes or undermine their morale. *Literary Gazette*, an official Soviet newspaper, reported after the Games: "A team of professional American spies and provocateurs tried to subvert the Russian sportsmen by attempting kidnappings, sneak-thievery and frame-ups on espionage charges.... American agents tried to palm off 'secret documents' on our girls and boys. They tried to give them photographs of military objectives in order to convict them later of espionage.... The American intelligence service did its utmost to force upon Soviet athletes an acquaintance with young women. Its agents more than insistently importuned them to 'have a good time.'"

As it turned out, the Soviets had a very good time indeed: They left Melbourne with 98 medals versus just 74 for the runner-up Americans. No other nation came close.

Fierce though the clash between the superpowers was, the most ferocious political confrontation in Melbourne occurred in a water polo match between Hungary and Russia. Earlier in the fall, bands of brave Hungarian freedom fighters had risen up against Soviet oppression. Underequipped though they were, the ragged rebels still made enough trouble that the Soviets thought it imperative to crush them with tanks and troops, taking control of Budapest just 18 days before the Olympics began. The Hungarian-Soviet water

Blankers-Koen was the star of the London Games in '48.

polo game became an extension of the battle back in Europe with above-water punching and under-water fouling that resulted in bloodshed and put a pro-Hungarian crowd on the brink of riot. The Hungarian team beat the Soviets 4–0 and, to the delight of the free world, went on to win the gold medal.

The individual star of the Melbourne Games was not a cold war surrogate of any kind but a blue-eyed Australian teenager who ran like the wind with a halo of blonde curls bouncing on her head. Betty Cuthbert was just 18, but she won three gold medals: in the 100- and 200-meter dashes and the 400-meter relay. Instantly dubbed the Golden Girl, she was wined and dined by appreciative Aussies all across the land, but being a national heroine was not for her. "I detested being a public figure," she said later. "I suppose it was because I was only 18. I think I get more of a thrill out of those three gold medals now when I read the old clippings than I did at the time. But I hated the attention. I wanted to quit." The Golden Girl did not quit for good for a long time—not even after the Games in 1960, when she failed to medal. She went on to Tokyo in 1964 where she astonished everyone by winning another gold in the 400-meter run at the age of 26. She recalled, "In Melbourne it had happened so quickly, I hadn't time to think of it. But in Tokyo the fact I had won came over me right away. I felt it inside. It was splendid."

The Winter Games of 1960 were held in the Sierra Nevada hamlet of Squaw Valley, California. The opening ceremonies and general all-around pageantry were under the supervision of none other than Walt Disney, who imported a 2,600-voice choir, a 1,500-piece band and Vice-President Richard Nixon for the big show. But all this wasn't enough to give the American Olympians a victory, even in their own backyard: The Soviets won 21 medals to the U.S.'s paltry 10. One of those 10, however, was produced by an inspired young hockey team that upset the mighty Soviets—a miracle on ice that, miraculously enough, was to be repeated in another American hamlet 20 years later.

The Summer Games of 1960 opened against an odd and anomalous backdrop that combined the classic architecture of ancient Rome with a chilling, very contemporary cold war drama of tension and distrust. The Soviets had shot down an American U-2 spy plane and captured its pilot just three months before the Games began, thereby dashing the hopes for a summit conference between President Eisenhower and Premier Khrushchev. For a time the world seemed balanced on the brink of disaster. Perhaps in frightened recognition of the danger, an extraordinary amount of fraternizing developed between East and West as the Rome Games progressed. At one point the chairman of the Soviet Olympic Committee, Constantin Andrianov, actually said, "Politics is one thing, sport another. We are sportsmen."

Still, when it was all over, the Soviets did not hesitate to remind the world that their political ideology was clearly superior to all others because they had won 103 medals to the U.S.'s 71.

Of course, politicical ideology was far from being uppermost in the mind of your average Olympic medal winner. No one testified to this better than the American pole vaulter Don Bragg, who won the gold in Rome and was surely one of the more idiosyncratic individuals ever to invade an Olympic venue. A very beefy, very talkative citizen of Penns Grove, New Jersey, Bragg recalled: "To get to the Olympics I lived like a monk when I was in college. Vaulting was my life.... I hardly went out with girls until I was 20.... I lived on skim milk and honey for 10 years because if I went over 200 pounds—*crackkkk!*—the poles would go. The Olympics were like a religious pilgrimage.... I won the gold medal after eight hours of vaulting. Eight hours! Jesus, I'd dropped from 198 to 187 pounds, but I won, and I let go with this fantastic Tarzan yell. It echoed all over the stadium. The crowd went wild. The Italians loved it!"

The Hungary–U.S.S.R. water polo match led to bloodshed in '56.

The Tarzan yell, as it turned out, was hardly a spontaneous inspiration: "All I ever really wanted to be was Tarzan. It was my dream and my obsession.... I won the gold medal in Rome because I wanted to be Tarzan.... The gold medal did it for me; Hollywood called. I moved out there to be Tarzan. They wanted to straighten my nose and cut my vocal cords. My wife was about to have our first baby, and she went home to New Jersey. I was living with Horace Heidt, the bandleader, and one night I took this girl home from some party and some guy took a shot at me. God, the headlines! And then I got to thinking about what the hell am I doing in Hollywood? What the hell am I doing with nose jobs and voice box fixes? I figured it's all too rich for my blood, so I came home."

Later Bragg had a couple of chances to play Tarzan in the movies and on television, but they fell through, and he was left with his gold medal and his hopes—none of which involved East-West politics. "Ever since the Olympics, everything in life has been anticlimactic," he said. "If I lived in Europe, I would be a millionaire. So would Parry O'Brien or Rafer Johnson [decathlon winner in Rome].... They know all of us over there—we're celebrities. Here in the States it's always, 'Hey, Don, drop by and see us when you're through competing. We might have something real good for ya.' But when you do drop by, it's always, 'Hey, jeez, Don, I'm sorry, but we're all filled up, man.' I thought about going into teaching, but I didn't because I didn't want people pointing at me and saying, 'Hey, he's an Olympic champion, and he's only making eight grand a year.'"

The cold war dragged on for another 30 years after the Rome Olympics. Through it all, politicians and patriots from East and West alike continued to insist that Olympic medal winners—including the likes of the magnificently screwball Tarzan wannabe from Penns Grove—should stand as symbols of the success or failure of a political ideology. The absurdity of it all never seemed to register with the scorekeepers on either side.

FANNY BLANKERS-KOEN
(ABOVE) RAN FOR THE GOLD
IN THE 100-METER DASH,
ONE OF HER FOUR
VICTORIES IN LONDON;
MICHELINE OSTERMEYER
COLLECTED A PAIR OF GOLDS
IN THE SHOT PUT AND
DISCUS; AND SAMMY LEE
(FAR RIGHT) WAS THE
PLATFORM DIVING
CHAMPION

BENCHMARKS

JANUARY
Mahatma Gandhi
is assassinated
by a Hindu
extremist.

APRIL
The U.S. defies a
Soviet blockade
by airlifting
supplies to
Berlin.

APRIL
Humphrey Bogart
stars in John
Huston's *Treasure
of the Sierra Madre*.

MAY
Israel becomes
an independent
nation.

AUGUST
Babe Ruth dies
of cancer.

OCTOBER
Mao Tse-tung and
his Communist
forces take over
Manchuria.

NOVEMBER
Harry Truman
baffles the experts
by defeating
Thomas Dewey in
the presidential
election.

ST. MORITZ **1948**

ST. MORITZ PROVIDED A PICTURE-PERFECT
SETTING FOR WINTER GAMES SUCH AS HOCKEY (RIGHT), AS
WELL AS FOR OTHER ICE CAPADES LIKE DICK BUTTON'S
AERIAL BALLET (ABOVE), WHICH HELPED HIM WIN THE
FIRST OF TWO CONSECUTIVE GOLD MEDALS
IN MEN'S FIGURE SKATING

1952

HELSINKI
OSLO

THE COLD WAR FOUND A NEW BATTLEFIELD IN THE

OLYMPIC GAMES, AND ALL OF A SUDDEN ATHLETES WERE REDUCED TO

THE STATUS OF POLITICAL PAWNS. IT WAS NOT THE

LAST TIME THEY WERE SO USED—NOR THE LAST TIME THEY

ROSE ABOVE SUCH CONSIDERATIONS

THE ZATOPEKS WERE THE TOAST OF HELSINKI, AS DANA
(ABOVE) WON THE JAVELIN THROW AND EMIL WOWED THE
WORLD WITH GOLDS IN THE 5,000- AND 10,000-METER
RUNS AS WELL AS THE MARATHON (RIGHT)

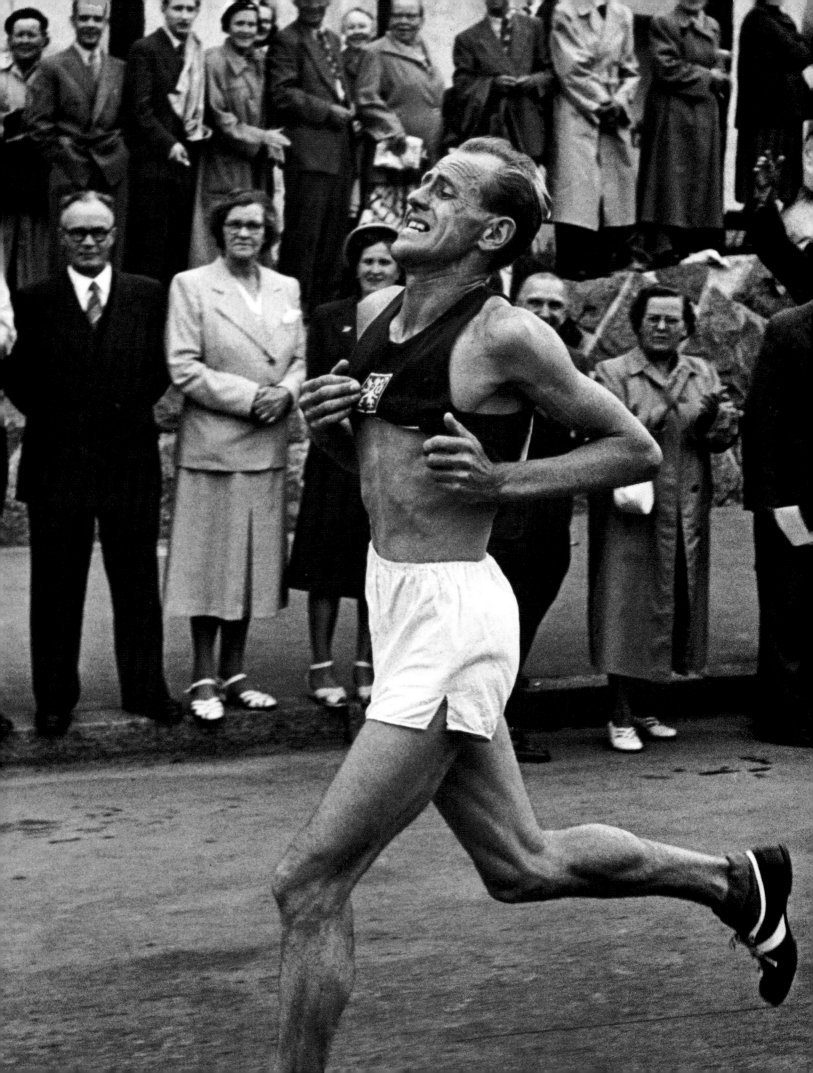

HELSINKI
1952

BOB MATHIAS (LEFT) OF THE U.S. WAS
DECATHLON CHAMPION AGAIN, THIS TIME WINNING
EASILY AND SETTING A WORLD RECORD IN
THE PROCESS; FELLOW AMERICAN PAT MCCORMICK (ABOVE)
WON THE GOLD MEDAL IN BOTH THE PLATFORM
AND THE SPRINGBOARD DIVING EVENTS,
A DOUBLE THAT SHE REPEATED FOUR YEARS
LATER IN MELBOURNE

DICK BUTTON (ABOVE) SOARED TO ANOTHER GOLD MEDAL IN FIGURE SKATING, WHILE ANDREA MEAD LAWRENCE (FAR RIGHT), WHO HAD ALREADY WON A GOLD IN THE GIANT SLALOM, OVERCAME A FALL ON HER FIRST SLALOM RUN AND WENT ON TO VICTORY, BECOMING THE FIRST U.S. SKIER TO WIN TWO GOLD MEDALS; DESPITE THEIR 16-YEAR-OLD BOBSLED, ANDREAS OSTLER (RIGHT, SEATED) AND LORENZ NIEBERL STREAKED DOWN THE COURSE TO A DOMINANT WIN IN THE TWO-MAN EVENT

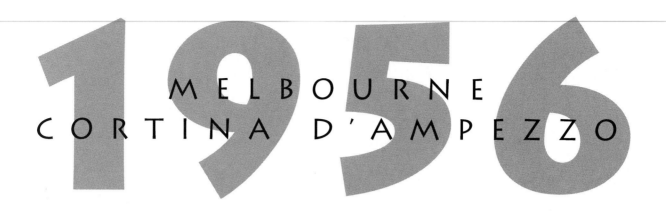

1956
MELBOURNE
CORTINA D'AMPEZZO

THE POLITICS OF THE COLD WAR CONTINUED TO

INFECT THE OLYMPICS AS THE SOVIETS ENGINEERED THE FIRST IN A LONG

LINE OF DOMINANT OUTCOMES, LEADING ALL NATIONS IN MEDALS IN BOTH

THE SUMMER AND WINTER GAMES. THE U.S. AND THE REST OF THE WEST

STRUGGLED TO KEEP PACE

BETWEEN 1956 AND 1964, SOVIET GYMNAST AND
ALL-AROUND CHAMPION LARISSA LATYNINA WOULD WIN A
RECORD 18 MEDALS; BETTY CUTHBERT (RIGHT) OF AUSTRALIA
WAS THE LOCAL HERO, WITH THREE SPRINTING GOLDS

BOBBY MORROW
(ABOVE) OF THE U.S. BECAME
THE FIRST MAN SINCE
JESSE OWENS IN 1936 TO RUN
FOR GOLD IN BOTH SPRINTS;
T. PETER RADEMACHER
(RIGHT) KNOCKED DOWN
SOVIET LEV MUKHIN THREE
TIMES IN THE FIRST ROUND
FOR THE HEAVYWEIGHT
GOLD; POLAND'S ELZBIETA
KRZESINSKA (FAR RIGHT)
SOARED FOR GOLD IN
THE LONG JUMP

CORTINA D'AMPEZZO **1956**

TONI SAILER OF AUSTRIA (ABOVE), DESPITE A
BROKEN BOOTSTRAP JUST MINUTES BEFORE
THE START OF THE DOWNHILL, BECAME THE FIRST SKIER
TO WIN GOLD MEDALS IN ALL THREE ALPINE
EVENTS—THE SLALOM, GIANT SLALOM AND DOWNHILL;
TENLEY ALBRIGHT OF THE U.S. (RIGHT) TOOK THE FIGURE
SKATING GOLD MEDAL, THEN WENT ON TO MEDICAL
SCHOOL AND A CAREER AS A SURGEON

1960

ROME
SQUAW VALLEY

HEIGHTENED TENSION GRIPPED THE OLYMPICS WHEN THE

SOVIETS DOWNED AN AMERICAN SPY PLANE IN THE INTERVAL

BETWEEN THE WINTER AND SUMMER GAMES, BUT THE ATHLETES RESPONDED

WITH MEMORABLE PERFORMANCES AND A SPIRIT OF GOODWILL THAT

TRANSCENDED RACE AND NATIONAL BOUNDARIES

**WILMA RUDOLPH, FORMER POLIO VICTIM, ELECTRIFIED THE
GAMES WITH GOLDS IN BOTH SPRINTS; JERRY WEST (RIGHT)
LED A DOMINANT U.S. BASKETBALL TEAM—10 OF ITS 12
MEMBERS ENDED UP IN THE NBA—ON AN OLYMPIC ROMP**

ROME 1960

A BRASH YOUNG MAN NAMED CASSIUS CLAY
GRABBED HIS FIRST NATIONAL ATTENTION—IT WOULD
HARDLY BE HIS LAST—BY WINNING A GOLD MEDAL IN
BOXING'S LIGHT HEAVYWEIGHT DIVISION; ABEBE BIKILA DID
NOT TALK NEARLY SO MUCH, BUT HIS REMARKABLE
BAREFOOT TRIUMPH IN THE MARATHON (RIGHT) SPOKE
VOLUMES ABOUT HIS COURAGE, A QUALITY HE WOULD
DISPLAY AGAIN FOUR YEARS LATER WHEN HE BECAME THE
FIRST MAN TO WIN BACK-TO-BACK MARATHONS

WHILE A SMATTERING OF
FANS ENJOYED THE SEDATE
PAIRS COMPETITION (FAR
RIGHT), MANY MORE WERE
THRILLED BY THE
MIRACULOUS GOLD MEDAL
FOR THE U.S HOCKEY TEAM,
WHICH OVERCAME A 4–3
DEFICIT AGAINST
CZECHOSLOVAKIA IN ITS
FIRST GAME (ABOVE), AND
BY THE FIGURE SKATING
TRIUMPH OF
CAROL HEISS (RIGHT), WHO
DEDICATED HER
GOLD MEDAL TO HER
LATE MOTHER

AGAIN AND AGAIN OVER THE years, her photograph appeared in the Dutch newspapers: pedaling toward a workout with her two children riding in the basket of her bicycle or practicing the high jump while the kids played in the sand pit beneath her. She won five events in the Dutch championships in 1946 even though she had to hurry home between competitions to breast-feed her five-month-old daughter. Nevertheless, she was no heroine to women in those far-off times. Indeed, Francina Elsje

(Fanny) Blankers-Koen (pronounced Koon) was an object of widespread disapproval for stealing so much time for sports from her proper responsibilities as wife, mother and homemaker. In fact, she said that she managed to train only twice a week "between washing dishes and darning socks."

After an unsatisfying appearance as a raw 18-year-old at the 1936 Games in Berlin (where her best result was a fifth in the 400-meter relay), Blankers-Koen had to sit out the war-canceled Games of '40 and '44. Finally, in 1948, when she was 30, she was able to compete at the London Olympics. When she and her husband-coach Jan Blankers went to London, they left the children in Amsterdam with Fanny's father, who promised her, "Win, and I will dance around the kitchen table."

Everyone assumed she was too old to do well, but she entered *five* events—the 100- and 200-meter dashes, 80-meter hurdles, 400-meter relay and the long jump. The 100 came first, with the finals held in a needlelike rain. After she had won by a comfortable margin of five feet, she quickly sought out a microphone held by a Dutch broadcaster and sent an exuberant message home: "Poppa! Dance now around the kitchen table!"

Unfortunately, the qualifying heats for the 80-meter hurdles and the long jump were set for the same day, and Blankers-Koen was forced to pass on the long jump in favor of the hurdles. It proved to be an ugly, unsettling race in which almost everything went wrong for her. She had slept little and was extremely tense. The starter's pistol didn't fire—and then it did. Blankers-Koen lost her rhythm and started a step behind her chief rival, a 19-year-old

British ballet teacher named Maureen Gardner. Blankers-Koen caught up at the second hurdle, then at the fifth hurdle she took off late, hit the top bar and began to stumble. "What happened then is a blurred memory," she recalled later. "My style went to pieces, and I staggered in like a drunkard." She felt the tape slap her forehead, but she also saw both Gardner and a young Australian, Shirley Strickland, cross the line in what looked like a dead heat. No one knew who had won, and the contestants waited nervously as judges scrutinized finish-line photos. Suddenly the band struck up *God Save the King*, and Blankers-Koen sagged, assuming the British anthem signaled Gardner's victory. As it turned out, it merely marked the arrival of King George VI at the royal box, and a few minutes later Blankers-Koen was declared the gold medal winner with an Olympic-record time of 11.2 seconds.

All this left her an emotional wreck. On the day of the 200-meter heats, alone in the women's locker room, she sobbed inconsolably until finally a sympathetic attendant let her husband in to see her. Fanny told Jan she wanted to quit and go home. He paused, then said calmly, "If you don't want to go on, you must not. But I'm afraid you will be sorry later if you don't run." Of course she ran and won her third gold by a margin of seven yards—the greatest victory spread ever in a women's Olympic 200-meters. The next day she was victorious for the fourth time, overcoming a seemingly insurmountable five-yard deficit on the anchor leg of the 400-meter relay.

Blankers-Koen did not fully retire from competition until she was 37. When the women's movement wanted to celebrate her as a feminist heroine, she rejected the role. "Oh no, oh no," she said in 1985, "I don't like the word. Feminists … they want to work, they want the husband to do the housekeeping. I don't like that stuff.…Women can do a lot, of couse, but it's still not the same as being a man."

OLYMPIC RESUME: *With her triumphs in London in 1948, Fanny Blankers-Koen became the only woman to win four track and field gold medals at a single Olympics.*

DICK BUTTON

THE YEAR WAS 1941. THE neophyte figure skater was 12, a clumsy, unappealing tub of a child, 5'2" and 162 pounds, and his instructor dismissed him brutally: "You'll never learn to skate—not until hell freezes over." In the years after that, Dick Button won so many figure skating championships and was described so many times as "devilishly handsome" that one can be excused for wondering if that poor little klutz on skates cut some kind of Faustian deal in exchange for his transformation.

If such a bargain *was* struck with the devil, it came to fruition between 1946 and 1952, when this lithe ex-butterball won seven U.S. championships, one European, three North American, five world and two Olympic gold medals—thus becoming the first American male ever to win a gold in figure skating. He also introduced new elements that changed the face of the sport. He is still considered the only modern skater whose influence rivals that of Sonja Henie. Although figure skating is notoriously cluttered with arcane terminology—double Axels, triple toe loops, flying camels, etc.—Button himself cut through the jargon to describe the essence of his contribution: "My skating was athletic, and I changed the style. It was really an American style. Brash. It was the beginning of a 10-year period in which Americans dominated the sport."

His gold medal at the 1948 Games in St. Moritz was followed a week later by a world championship in Davos, Switzerland, and then by a European tour to show off his energetic new American style. He was greeted by ovations almost everywhere. One exception was Prague, which had fallen to Communist armed forces just before Button held his exhibition. As he entered the rink he was greeted by a barrage of oranges. "I thought this was the Czech version of an anti-American raspberry," he recalled, "and I threw the first orange off the rink. However, when others were thrown, I picked one up and noticed the paper in which it was wrapped had some encouraging words written on it: GOOD LUCK, U.S.A. Another said, COME ON, BUTTON!"

Back home he was besieged with offers to skate professionally, but he entered Harvard in the fall of '48 and refused all monetary temptation. "It's hard to convince people that finishing my studies and winning in the Olympics again mean much more to me than the professional propositions I've received. But they do," he said. By the time of his gold medal at the Oslo Games in 1952, Button had reached a point of competitive self-assurance that bordered on arrogance. "I can't copy anybody because nobody has done anything new," he said. "I don't worry about whom I am competing with. I skate against perfection."

That year Button also won the U.S. and world titles, got his undergraduate degree from Harvard cum laude, enrolled in Harvard Law School and signed with the Ice Capades for $150,000. After three months of commuting between Harvard and Madison Square Garden, he came down with mononucleosis and hepatitis. He quit skating, finished law school, then embarked on a career that had little or nothing to do with either ice or torts. He became an actor, appearing in *Pal Joey, Mister Roberts, On the Town, Call Me Madam* and co-starring in a 1958 NBC-TV spectacular called—what else?—*Hans Brinker and the Silver Skates*, with Tab Hunter and Basil Rathbone. He later looked back with understandable satisfaction on all this, saying, "I really think I did it right. So many kids drop out of school and spend all their time skating and become one-dimensional.... It was always fun for me, and there was quite a bit of the big ham in me."

In recent years Button has stayed close to the hambone as an uncommonly lucid commentator for ABC-TV's figure skating coverage and as the originator of one of the most successful of all TV trash-sport properties—*Superstars*—which pits outstanding athletes against each other in events outside their specialties.

All in all a devilishly clever career, you could say.

OLYMPIC RESUME: *Dick Button won gold medals in the men's Olympic figure skating competitions in 1948 and 1952. His victory in Oslo was among the most lopsided in Olympic history.*

HE STARTED COMPETING AT A late age for a distance runner, nearly 19, and he didn't do it by choice: "I was working in a shoe factory in Zlin, where I was born. The director of the factory said one day that there would be a race through the city on Sunday, and that I should run. I did not want to go. I told him I had a cold. I told him I had a bad knee. He made me go to the company doctor. The doctor said I was fine. I had to run. I surprised myself. I finished second."

That was in 1941, a hopeless time for serious sports competition of any kind in Czechoslovakia thanks to the war and the Nazi occupation. So Emil Zátopek competed with himself, running in place in his bathtub, running the steps of stadiums, running with a gas mask to help control his breathing. After the war the new Czechoslovakian army drafted him and told him that his military duty was to be a runner. Thus, Zátopek became an "amateur" athlete, socialist style.

Not many western journalists had seen him compete before London in 1948, and they were both amazed and amused by his grotesque behavior during a race. Red Smith wrote a memorable description: "This gaunt and grimacing Czech with the running form of a zombie had made himself the pinup boy of the London Games. Witnesses who have long since forgotten the other events still wake up screaming in the dark when Emil the Terrible goes writhing through their dreams, gasping, groaning, clawing at his abdomen in horrible extremities of pain." Zátopek, himself, was amused by his contortions, but he couldn't make himself run differently: "Other athletes come to me and say, 'Emil, it is horrible to see you run. Track and field is culture of natural movement, not this.' But I was interested in my finish, not in being beautiful."

Of course many of his finishes were beautiful beyond belief. He set 18 world records in just six years, won a gold in the 10,000 and a silver in the 5,000 in London, and, in a phenomenal series of races at the Helsinki Olympics in 1952, won golds in the 5,000, the 10,000 and the marathon—a race he had never before entered. In early 1991 he talked to Julie Cart of the *Los Angeles Times*

about that legendary victory: "The main coach of our team, he tried to warn me. 'You never run a marathon. You don't know pace, tactics.' But, for me, no problem." Zátopek read in the newspapers that Jim Peters of Great Britain was considered the likely winner, and on the day of the race he introduced himself. "I said, 'You are Peters? I am Zátopek, Czechoslovakia. Very glad to meet you.'... He must know how to run if he is favorite, so for me, it is only to keep up with him." Peters started very rapidly, and Zátopek kept up for a time. Eventually he politely inquired of the Englishman if perhaps his pace wasn't a bit too fast. Annoyed, Peters snapped that it was in fact too slow.

Zátopek fell back for a while, then passed Peters, who was in agony after his fiery early pace. As the marathon route looped out into the Finnish countryside, Zátopek moved far ahead of the field. He wasn't quite sure where he was, and he was in pain. "The only thing I can see ahead is a very high tower with a flame on top, the Olympic flame," he told Cart. "So I decide I must run to the flame." He won by 2½ minutes over the runner-up, and when someone asked him how he felt, he replied drolly, "The marathon is a very boring race."

At 34, Zátopek began to train for another Olympic marathon, in Melbourne. But after suffering a hernia from one of his unorthodox training techniques, doctors warned him he could not run for two months following surgery. The Olympics were too near to wait that long, and Zátopek began training the day after he left the hospital. Incredibly, he finished sixth in Melbourne—and that was the end of his Olympic heroics.

At the age of 70, in 1991, he was unable to run at all because of a sciatic nerve condition in his left leg. But he was still cheerful and optimistic. "I have more memories than most men," he said.

OLYMPIC RESUME: *Emil Zátopek won gold medals in the 10,000-meter run in 1948 and the 5,000- and 10,000-meter runs as well as the marathon in 1952, a triple that will probably never be matched.*

TWO YEARS AFTER 20-YEAR-old Toni Sailer won three gold medals in Alpine ski racing at the 1956 Winter Games in Cortina, Italy, Austrians were asked to rank the people who had done the most for their country in its 1,000-year history. Sailer, who installed windows and eave spouts before his Olympic triumphs, finished fifth, just behind Wolfgang Amadeus Mozart.

Soon after the Games, his mother had issued a widely reported ultimatum: "Toni has won enough gilded medals. It's time he made some money." Sailer happily set out to comply. After Cortina, the grateful villagers of Kitzbühel gave him the land on which to build a 32-bed inn, which was soon booked solid through the winters. His autobiography, *Mein Weg zum dreifachen Olympia-Sieg* (roughly: "How I Won the Triple Crown") sold 160,000 copies in German, 30,000 in Japanese and 10,000 in French. He also promoted a new plastic-fiberglass ski, made a few records as a shaky-voiced crooner and invested in a firm that produced Sailer-Tex, an elastic material used in ski pants.

But his real fortune, he hoped, was going to come from that most glamorous of professions: the movies. His first film, *Black Lightning,* was about a skier who spurns the amorous advances of a rich girl in order to marry the daughter of a local innkeeper. The critics were harsh, and Sailer himself was not happy with his leaden performance on the silver screen. "It was like when you hear what you think is your deep voice on a tape recorder, and it comes out high and squeaky," he said. He made some changes in his technique, but apparently not enough to satisfy the critics, who also panned his next two films—*Twelve Girls and a Man,* in which he played a border guard who finds 12 pretty girls on vacation in a mountain hut, and *A Thousand Stars Shine,* in which he played a garage mechanic who gets the girl after an auto accident.

After four months of work with a celebrated acting coach in Berlin to polish his technique and lighten his dense Tyrolean accent, Sailer went to Japan to shoot *King of the Silvery Summits.* It was a soapy saga in which he

played a ski champion who is accused of causing a fatal accident in Europe, flees to Japan, falls in love with a Japanese girl, is ultimately cleared of all charges and returns to Europe to win in the Olympic Games. To the Japanese it didn't matter how thick or hickish Sailer's German was: They adored him. Gangs of teenage girls hounded his every step, even forcing him to hide in his hotel bathroom one night, and there were police escorts and Japanese-style ticker tape parades everywhere he went to promote the film. *King of the Silvery Summits* drew 1.5 million fans in Japan.

All of this boosted his reputation in Europe, and he went home to star in *The White Dream,* in which he played a hockey goalie who falls in love with a figure skater. The film did fairly well, and Sailer spent the '60s acting in movies and stage productions such as *Death of a Salesman* and *The Moon Is Blue.* He did a TV series that he described as being "a lot like *Bonanza.*" But not enough like *Bonanza,* apparently— the show was short-lived. Even the luster of his Olympic triple triumph began to fade when a glamorous Frenchman, Jean-Claude Killy, also won three golds, at Grenoble in 1968. Sailer had finally become an object of trivia pursuers: "Who besides Killy won three...?"

Then, in 1972, Sailer experienced a resurrection in ski racing circles when he was appointed the head coach of a badly demoralized Austrian team, which had fallen on hard times. Though the ski world was skeptical about how well a glamour boy movie star would deal with a collection of cranky athletes and a hypercritical Austrian ski hierarchy, Sailer pulled the team out of its doldrums and made it into one of the finest ski teams of the 1970s. He retired from coaching in 1976 to raise his family and manage the inn in Kitzbühel. If a poll were taken today, Mozart would be in no danger of being overtaken by Toni Sailer.

OLYMPIC RESUME: *With victories in 1956 in the giant slalom, slalom and downhill, Toni Sailer became the first man to win gold medals in all three Olympic Alpine events.*

WILMA RUDOLPH

SHE WAS THE 20TH OF 22 children sired through two marriages by her father, a railroad porter and handyman in Clarksville, Tennessee. She was born prematurely, weighing just 4½ pounds, and her parents feared she would not survive. She did, but she was a vulnerable, sickly child, and when she was four she suffered a two-pronged attack of double pneumonia and scarlet fever. The assault left her with a crippled leg, which doctors predicted would never be normal. She

spent her childhood in steel braces and orthopedic shoes, enduring hot-water treatments and painful massages. The leg improved very slowly, until at last, when she was 12, the braces came off. "I was healthy all over my body for the first time," she recalled. "I felt at that point that my life was beginning at last. That summer I went over to a playground in town, and all the kids were around, playing a game called basketball."

Miraculously, within four years Wilma Glodean Rudolph became a superstar in both basketball and track. At 16 she tied for first place in the 200-meter dash in the Olympic trials and was selected to compete with the U.S. team at the 1956 Games in Melbourne. She was still quite childlike. Her nickname was Skeeter, short for mosquito; she had a spindly adolescent physique—very tall (nearly six feet) and very, very thin (89 pounds). In Melbourne she lost in a 200-meter heat and fell into a teenage funk over being "a failure." However, she restored her sense of self-esteem by winning a bronze medal with the 400-meter relay team.

She returned to high school in Tennessee, starred on the state championship basketball team as a junior and began spending more time with her boyfriend, another star athlete named Robert Eldridge. In the winter of 1958, Wilma made a devastating discovery: She was pregnant. Just 17 and mortified, she was relieved when her parents and coaches promised full support. She had to quit the basketball team and forgo the track season, but life went on. "At the end of May 1958," she recalled, "I graduated from high school; I was seven months pregnant. I went up and

took all the honors just like everyone else. In those days abortions were unheard of, and nobody was sent away to live with an aunt like the white girls. The black girls stayed in school pregnant, like nothing was wrong at all." Her baby, Yolanda, was born in July. Six weeks later the baby went to live with Wilma's married sister in St. Louis, and Wilma entered Tennessee State on an athletic scholarship.

In the U.S. team trials for the Rome Olympics in 1960, she qualified for the 100-meter dash, the 400-meter relay and the 200-meter dash, which she won in a stunning 22.9 seconds—the first time a woman had broken the 23-second barrier. In Rome, on the day before her opening heat in the 100, she stepped into a hole on a field near the Stadio Olimpico and twisted her ankle. "I heard it pop.... I was crying because the ankle hurt very badly, and I thought that I had broken it," she recalled. "The trainer took one look and made this horrible face. He immediately ordered some ice, and he packed it, and they carried me back to my room." It proved to be a sprain, and, tightly taped, the ankle held up so well that she tied the world record of 11.3 seconds in a heat and went on to victory in the final by an astonishing three yards.

Within six days she had won two more golds—in the 200-meter dash and the 400-meter relay—and became the most celebrated Olympian in Rome, rewarded with many fond nicknames—*La Perle Noire* and *La Chattanooga Choo Choo* by the French, *La Gazzella Nera* by the Italians, Wilma-on-the-Wing by the British. She retired from track a year after the Olympics, married Robert, became involved in the burgeoning U.S. civil rights movement, had three more children and went into business. At one point she operated under a most appropriate corporate name: Wilma Unlimited.

OLYMPIC RESUME: *Wilma Rudolph won gold medals in the 400-meter relay and the 100- and 200-meter dashes at the 1960 Olympics in Rome, making her one of only three women to sweep the three sprint events.*

AL OERTER

FOUR GOLD MEDALS IN FOUR consecutive Olympics are not won without agony, and Al Oerter could tick off his various points of pain as a tour guide does historical landmarks: "In Rome in 1960 the nervous tension was so bad it was like physical pain. I injured my neck in 1962 and had to wear a brace. In Tokyo in '64, I ripped the cartilage in my rib cage. I had to use novocaine. I was wrapped up in bandages like a mummy, but the pain was still fierce, and I was popping ammonia capsules to clear my head. In Mexico I pulled an abductor muscle in my leg a week before the Games.... It's the worst thing that can happen to a discus thrower. I couldn't make an involuntary left turn."

Despite all of the agony, he was consistently heroic in his performances, for he always came from behind. Not once in his four Olympic victories was he favored to win, and not once was he the reigning world-record holder, yet each time he set an Olympic record. After Mexico City in '68, where he won for the last time with a mighty throw of 212' 6"—more than five feet farther than he had ever flung the discus before—he decided he had done everything he could in his sport. "I think the best thing for me to do is to slide out of this gracefully," he said.

He started working out again to prepare for the 1972 Olympics, but in the winter of 1971 he added up the cost and reluctantly decided, again, that he must quit. "My neck was hurting, and I couldn't double my weightlifting program to put on the weight I needed, O.K.? I weigh 235 pounds, and I had to get it up to 275 or maybe 300 pounds to compete properly. I don't believe in steroids, and I think I've proved you don't have to take them. It's no secret that most of the weight guys used steroids in Tokyo and in Mexico, but I don't believe in them, O.K.?"

Still, he couldn't resist trying again, for the Montreal Games in 1976. This time he did try steroids for a couple of months. "I wanted to put on some bulk, and a physician put me on a light program. But it caused my blood pressure to go through the ceiling and made no difference at all in my performance. It's all in the mind." He blamed the drugs for a new "abrasiveness" he sensed in his sport. "When I left in 1968," he said, "everybody was fairly good friends. But when I came back, no one spoke. People were locked in mortal combat in the discus event. This is combat? The attitudes just drove me nuts."

Oerter wasn't able to get himself ready in time for Montreal but, amazingly enough, he did manage to put himself in competitive condition again—sans steroids— for the Moscow Games of 1980. He was 43. Then President Jimmy Carter orchestrated a 62-nation boycott of the Moscow Olympics in retaliation for the Soviet invasion of Afghanistan. At first Oerter was outraged: "There was no way in hell I wasn't going, regardless. All I could think of were the hours and hours of training and sacrifice—out the window. I wanted the U.S. to show off its strength the way the Czechs did in 1968 and the Hungarians in 1956. I wanted to go to Moscow and knock their jocks off."

But two days later he did a complete about-face: "My conscience overcame me." He testified before Congress: "By not participating we can raise a question in the mind of Soviet citizens that something is not right." Many of his would-be teammates were furious at him and pointed out that it was easier for Oerter to back the boycott because neither his livelihood nor his self-esteem relied completely on athletic competition. He was at the time manager of data communications at Grumman Data Systems, a company for which he had worked for more than 20 years.

In a very real sense, Al Oerter was the last of a nearly extinct breed—an old-fashioned, independent, self-reliant Olympic puritan: "I've always viewed it as recreation. I don't need a pot of gold to make me train hard. That's absurd for a discus thrower. You work four years for a medal and then throw it in a drawer. I was training for a lot of reasons, not the least of which was that I get a lot of fun out of seeing that damn thing fly."

OLYMPIC RESUME: *With victories in the discus throw in 1956, '60, '64 and '68, Al Oerter became the only man to win gold medals in four consecutive Olympics.*

HE ACCOMPLISHED SOMEthing no other runner ever had: He won the gold medal in two Olympic marathons. One victory came in the celebrated race in Rome in 1960 when he ran barefoot over the cobblestones of the Appian Way to break Emil Zátopek's Olympic record by nearly eight minutes. The other occurred in Tokyo in 1964 when he wore shoes and finished more than four minutes ahead of the runners-up, bettering his own Olympic mark by 4:05.

Abebe Bikila died in 1973 of a brain hemorrhage. He was only 41, and it was far too soon, far too sudden. But an early death was perhaps not the greatest tragedy visited on this noble fellow. Bikila, the first of the great East African runners, had spent the last four years of his life in a wheelchair, paralyzed from the waist down. He was crippled one night in the winter of 1969. He was driving on a dark, dirt road when he was blinded by the lights of an oncoming car. He swerved, overturned and, hours later, was found unconscious, crushed beneath his car. He was flown to England for treatment, but the paralysis proved irreversible, and less than a year later he returned to Addis Ababa. There he lived with his wife and four children in a sturdy wooden house with polished wood floors and walls lined with his trophies and hung with Ethiopian war shields. Surrounding the house was a seven-foot corrugated iron fence enclosing a bright green lawn where half a dozen sheep grazed among a flock of chickens.

Bikila was something of a holy man in the years between his paralysis and his death. Children and Ethiopian soldiers called on him frequently as did world-class runners, who made the trek to his home like disciples on a pilgrimage. Even before his accident, he had been treated like a god by his countrymen. As a journalist reported from Addis Ababa in the mid-1960s: "Only Emperor Haile Selassie has greater stature than Bikila among the Ethiopian people— and not much more…. Bikila walks the streets as a national hero. People cheer him wildly, but none would dare walk up and shake his hand or ask for his autograph—no more than they would approach the Emperor himself." Bikila's

victories in Rome and Tokyo, plus a third valiant attempt to win the marathon in Mexico City in 1968 (he dropped out with an injury), had produced plenty of material rewards, too—his house, a car and a very swift series of promotions from private to captain in the elite ranks of the emperor's guard.

Nevertheless, Bikila remained a purist in his dedication to the traditional Olympic credo that stood foursquare for amateurism and dead against the intrusion of politics. As for Olympians cashing in on commercial pursuits, he said, "An Olympic athlete is first an amateur who is going to compete for the flag of his country. Now and again a sportsman appears on the scene who seems unable to make the distinction between competing for his nation and gaining personal profit. Amateurs should not be paid—not to advertise products or anything else. I do not agree with any profit-making devices allied to the Olympics." As for politics, he was asked if his victory in Rome had been sweeter because it happened in Italy—a nation that had waged a brutal one-sided war against ill-armed Ethiopian troops in the 1930s. Bikila brushed the idea aside stiffly. "I think there must be a clear distinction between sport and politics. Sport is for international friendship. The Olympics have nothing to do with war—not with any war."

When Bikila was asked how a great runner faced life confined to a wheelchair, his face was impassive: "Men of success meet with tragedy. It was the will of God that I won the Olympics, and it was the will of God that I met with my accident. I was overjoyed when I won the marathon twice. But I accepted those victories as I accept this tragedy. I have no choice. I have to accept both circumstances as facts of life and live happily."

OLYMPIC RESUME: *With victories in Rome in 1960 and Tokyo in 1964, Abebe Bikila became the first man to win back-to-back Olympic marathons. Both of his winning times were world bests. In 1980, Waldemar Cierpinski of East Germany won his second consecutive Olympic marathon to equal Bikila's feat.*

HE WAS MODEST, HAND-some, dedicated to his parents, a mere schoolboy of 17, and his gold medal in the decathlon in London in 1948 stood as living proof that Jack Armstrong was alive and well and living in Tulare, California (pop. 13,000). One resident of the town gushed to a visiting journalist, "No matter who you are, you've got to like him.... If you were a mother or father, Bob's the kind of guy you'd want for a son; if you were a fellow, you'd want him for a chum, and if you were a girl — well, just look at the guy."

Later, as he began preparing for his second decathlon victory in Helsinki, there were the inevitable comparisons to the greatest athlete of them all, Jim Thorpe. A LIFE magazine writer who visited Thorpe in 1951 wrote, "At 63, broke and in poor health, the old Indian listened stolidly last week to tales about 20-year-old Bob Mathias.... Had Thorpe ever met Mathias? 'Just once,' he grunted. 'He's a nice kid, great track man. I don't know about his football.'" The LIFE man explained that Mathias was playing fullback for Stanford that year and that he recently had unleashed a "typically Thorpean, 96-yard touchdown run" to defeat USC. But "the old Indian," who had starred as a major league baseball player and professional football player, among many other things, was not impressed. "Mathias hasn't had a chance to play as many sports as I did," he said. "But even if he had, he probably wouldn't be as good as me."

Probably not. But in 1952, the competitive atmosphere Mathias found in Helsinki was more intense than anything Jim Thorpe had ever faced. The Soviets had come for the first time in more than 40 years, and the hostility of cold war politics permeated every event. As Mathias himself said later, "There were many more pressures on American athletes because of the Russians than in 1948. They were in a sense the real enemy. You just loved to beat 'em. You just had to beat 'em.... This feeling was strong down through the whole team, even members in sports where the Russians didn't excel." Mathias himself faced little competition from beyond the Iron Curtain,

with fourth-place finisher Vladimir Volkov the only Soviet to approach him in his triumphant march through the decathlon.

Mathias was still only 21. What next for the boy hero? Well, he was drafted by the Washington Redskins, who had planned to make him a wide receiver. But he decided to try show business instead, starring in a real-life sports-hero movie, *The Bob Mathias Story*. As it turned out, this box-office bomb effectively demolished his hopes for a third gold medal in Melbourne. In what can only be called a "typically Thorpean" move, the Amateur Athletic Union declared Mathias a pro, in part because he was paid to make the film. "At the time, I was terribly disappointed," Mathias recalled. "In 1956, I was still only 25. I was at my peak, still growing as an athlete."

That was the end of sports heroics for Bob Mathias. However, he continued to cash in on his fame, and from 1967 through 1974 he served as a conservative Republican congressman from California's 18th district. As he candidly declared while he was still in office, "Winning an Olympic gold medal helps in business or politics or anything.... Some people will vote for any name on the ballot that is familiar." Unfortunately, in the 1974 election Mathias's name was familiar to his constituents as that of a man who had voted against an amendment to a very popular aid-to-education bill, and they threw him out of Congress.

He has had a number of jobs since then — including California finance director of the Ford-for-President campaign and director of the U.S. Olympic Training Center in Colorado Springs. Currently he is president of the American Sports Kids Association, a California-based organization devoted to developing children's self-esteem through athletics. It has been years since anyone compared him to Jack Armstrong or Jim Thorpe.

OLYMPIC RESUME: *In 1948, at the age of 17, Bob Mathias became the youngest decathlon winner in Olympic history. Four years later he was victorious again, setting a world record and becoming the first man to win back-to-back gold medals in the event.*

1964-1976

THE GAMES GO GLOBAL

THE U.S. (ABOVE, FOREGROUND) SCORED A SURPRISING WIN OVER GERMANY IN THE EIGHT-OARED SHELL COMPETITION; PETER SNELL (FAR RIGHT) WON DOUBLE GOLD IN THE 800- AND 1,500-METER RUNS; WHILE BOB HAYES (RIGHT) STREAKED TO AN INCREDIBLE SEVEN-FOOT VICTORY IN THE 100-METER DASH

BENCHMARKS

FEBRUARY
The Beatles arrive
in New York City,
and the
British invasion is
under way.

FEBRUARY
Cassius Clay
defeats Sonny
Liston to become
the heavyweight
champion.

APRIL
Ford introduces the
Mustang.

APRIL
Sidney Poitier
becomes the first
black Oscar winner
for his performance
in *Lilies of the Field*.

JULY
LBJ signs the
Civil Rights Bill.

SEPTEMBER
The Warren
Commission
concludes
its investigation
into the death
of JFK.

DECEMBER
Martin Luther
King receives the
Nobel Peace Prize.

INNSBRUCK 1964

COMPETITORS IN THE SKI JUMP (LEFT) ENJOYED
A PANORAMIC VIEW OF INNSBRUCK, WHILE CLOSER TO
EARTH LYDIA SKOBLIKOVA (ABOVE) OF THE SOVIET UNION
GLIDED TO GOLD IN ALL FOUR WOMEN'S SPEED
SKATING EVENTS AND JEAN SAUBERT OF THE U.S. RECEIVED
KISSES FROM THE SISTERS GOITSCHELL, CHRISTINE (FAR
RIGHT) AND MARIELLE, AFTER THE GIANT SLALOM IN WHICH
MARIELLE TOOK THE GOLD AND CHRISTINE AND
SAUBERT TIED FOR THE SILVER

1968

MEXICO CITY
GRENOBLE

WHILE THE WINTER GAMES CELEBRATED A PAIR OF

DAZZLING STARS NAMED FLEMING AND KILLY, THE SUMMER VERSION

FEATURED A HEADY MIX OF RECORD-BREAKING PERFORMANCES

AND BITTER CONTROVERSY AS THE SPIRIT OF THE '60S INVADED THE

OLYMPIC VENUE FOR THE FIRST TIME

GEORGE FOREMAN'S FLAG-WAVING AFTER HIS GOLD MEDAL
IN HEAVYWEIGHT BOXING WAS NOT WELL RECEIVED BY CIVIL
RIGHTS ACTIVISTS; WORLD-RECORD-HOLDER BOB SEAGREN
(RIGHT) SOARED TO VICTORY IN THE POLE VAULT

MEXICO CITY
1968

FORGOTTEN IN THE FUROR OVER TOMMIE SMITH'S BLACK-POWER SALUTE ON THE VICTORY STAND WAS THE ASTONISHING PERFORMANCE THAT PRECEDED IT—HIS WORLD-RECORD TIME OF 19.83 IN THE 200-METER DASH (ABOVE) WOULD STAND FOR 11 YEARS; EVEN MORE DURABLE WAS BOB BEAMON'S SUPERHUMAN LONG JUMP (FAR RIGHT) THAT SHATTERED THE WORLD RECORD BY 21³/₄" AND REMAINED UNSURPASSED UNTIL 1991; GYMNAST VERA CASLAVSKA WON FOUR GOLDS, THEN BECAME A HEROINE IN CZECHOSLOVAKIA'S STRUGGLE AGAINST SOVIET DOMINATION

GRENOBLE **1968**

THE SUAVE JEAN-CLAUDE KILLY (ABOVE) OF
FRANCE SKIED TO GOLD MEDALS IN THE SLALOM, GIANT
SLALOM AND DOWNHILL, THEN WENT ON TO BECOME
AN INTERNATIONAL CELEBRITY; PEGGY FLEMING (RIGHT) OF
THE U.S. WAS THE OTHER STAR OF THE GAMES,
USING HER GRACEFUL ARTISTRY IN FIGURE SKATING TO
CAPTIVATE A GLOBAL AUDIENCE

128

BENCHMARKS

JANUARY
The Viet Cong launch the Tet offensive.

MARCH
LBJ announces that he will not run for reelection as president.

APRIL
Martin Luther King is assassinated in Memphis.

APRIL
The Prague Spring brings a new sense of freedom to Czechoslovakia.

JUNE
Robert Kennedy is assassinated in Los Angeles.

AUGUST
Soviet tanks invade Prague.

NOVEMBER
Richard Nixon is elected president.

DECEMBER
The Apollo 8 astronauts return home after becoming the first men to orbit the moon.

1972

MUNICH
SAPPORO

A SUCCESSFUL WINTER OLYMPICS AND A PASSEL

OF GLITTERING PERFORMANCES IN THE SUMMER FADED TO INSIGNIFICANCE

IN THE FACE OF THE HORRIFYING EVENTS IN MUNICH, WHERE

POLITICS INVADED THE GAMES WITH SHOCKING FORCE, LEAVING 11 ISRAELIS

DEAD AND A WORLD IN MOURNING

**THE FLAG STOOD AT HALF-MAST DURING THE MEMORIAL
SERVICE (ABOVE) FOR THE SLAIN ISRAELIS AS A SENSE
OF TRAGEDY OVERSHADOWED EVEN THE SEVEN GOLDS AND
SEVEN WORLD RECORDS OF MARK SPITZ (RIGHT)**

MUNICH
1972

WHILE GYMNAST OLGA KORBUT WAS ALL SMILES DURING HER GOLD MEDAL PERFORMANCE IN THE FLOOR EXERCISES (LEFT), THE U.S. BASKETBALL TEAM (ABOVE) WAS A STUDY IN DESPAIR AFTER ITS CONTROVERSIAL LOSS TO THE SOVIET UNION; DAN GABLE (TOP) TOOK THE GOLD IN WRESTLING'S LIGHTWEIGHT DIVISION, THEN WENT ON TO ESTABLISH AN NCAA DYNASTY AS A COACH AT IOWA

1976

MONTREAL
INNSBRUCK

INNSBRUCK HOSTED THE OLYMPICS FOR THE SECOND

TIME IN 12 YEARS AND PROVED YET AGAIN HOW CHARMING THE WINTER

GAMES CAN BE, BUT MONTREAL WAS NOT SO LUCKY—THE

SUMMER GAMES LEFT CANADIAN TAXPAYERS WITH A MASSIVE DEBT

THAT IS STILL BEING PAID TO THIS DAY

EAST GERMANY'S KORNELIA ENDER (ABOVE) HAD GOOD REASON
FOR CELEBRATION—SHE SWAM TO FOUR GOLD MEDALS;
BRUCE JENNER (RIGHT) WAS THE ALL-AMERICAN HERO, WITH
AN OVERWHELMING WIN IN THE DECATHLON

136

M O N T R E A L **1976**

TWO OF THE MOST ACCOMPLISHED PERFORMERS IN
OLYMPIC HISTORY TOOK CENTER STAGE IN MONTREAL:
NADIA COMANECI (RIGHT), WHO WON THREE GOLD MEDALS,
ONE SILVER AND ONE BRONZE WHILE POSTING
SEVEN 10'S, THE FIRST SUCH PERFECT SCORES EVER RECORDED
IN GYMNASTICS; AND LASSE VIREN (ABOVE), WHO
DOUBLED HIS DOUBLE OF 1972 BY WINNING THE 5,000-
AND 10,000-METER RUNS YET AGAIN

INNSBRUCK **1976**

FRANZ KLAMMER (LEFT) OF AUSTRIA FELL
BEHIND BERNHARD RUSSI'S TIME AT THE BEGINNING OF
HIS FINAL DOWNHILL RUN, THEN SURPASSED IT
WITH A RECKLESS CHARGE FOR THE GOLD MEDAL THAT SENT
THE HOMETOWN CROWD INTO DELIRIUM; THE
EAST GERMANS TRIUMPHED IN THE FOUR-MAN BOBSLED
(ABOVE) FOR THE FIRST OF THREE STRAIGHT GOLD
MEDALS THEY WOULD WIN IN THE EVENT

HE WAS THE ULTIMATE American Boy—blue eyes, blond hair, broad shoulders, radiant smile—and always a winner. His four gold medals won in Tokyo when he was just 18 were proof that the ideal red, white and blue kid really did exist. The fact that he was the first American since Jesse Owens in 1936 to win that many golds in one Olympics was testimony to how terrific the American system was in that it could produce two such admirable heroes from two such radically different backgrounds.

Don Schollander was voted the World's Best Athlete of 1964, won the Sullivan Award and was named Athlete of the Year by the Associated Press, beating out Johnny Unitas and Dean Chance for the prize. People wanted to know all about him, even his childhood, and his mother recalled for the press, "Everybody would come up to his carriage, see his blond curly hair and say, 'What a pretty little girl!'" His father, Wendell, was an insurance man who had been an honorable mention All-America halfback at North Dakota State.

After the Tokyo Games, young Schollander went to Yale, was elected to the secret society Skull and Bones and declared to the world that he was something more than a fast-moving object in water. "I don't call myself a swimmer at all. I'm a person who happens to swim," he told SPORTS ILLUSTRATED. Pressed to estimate exactly how important swimming was to him, Schollander said, "It would sound silly in quotes: 'Swimming is one forty-second of my life.' I don't sit around and talk about swimmers. I don't room with swimmers. I don't keep a workout diary or read swimming magazines."

The decade of the '60s was a time of cynicism and doubt among American youth, and it demanded a redefinition of values—even (or maybe especially) for clean-cut types like Schollander. He waded into the debate with enthusiasm: "We aren't as impressed with 'making it.' I'm certainly not a spokesman for my generation, but what's going on with today's youth is the concept of helping others—humanitarianism.... For example, I'm quite interested in doing extremely well financially in a relatively short time. I'm not money-hungry, but what I want to do is become financially secure so I can become more fully motivated to higher things in life—social good, humanitarian values."

He got off to an early start in the money-making department. After his freshman year at Yale, he came down with mononucleosis and had to spend the summer in bed at his family's home in Oregon. Bored, he began reading about the stock market in the newspapers. Soon he was studying corporate reports and playing the market on paper. At last he convinced his father to let him invest real money from his savings in the stock of an obscure firm he had been following. He bought Lear Jet at 32, watched it climb to 72 in a matter of months, then sold it when it began a downward trend.

He continued swimming through his Yale years, sometimes blowing his opponents out with sheer power, sometimes psyching them with his own assortment of poolside put-downs: "Some are naive," he explained, "like, 'I feel great. Boy, I'm going to have a good time.' Some are more sophisticated, like, 'God, I was watching your start. It's really interesting. I noticed that you start kicking before you get in the water. Doesn't it slow you down?'" At times he had trouble convincing himself that big-time competition was worth the great effort it required. "To take time out for the 1968 Olympics, this bothers me," he said.

But he did, and in Mexico City, he won only one gold and one silver medal. Of course, he had something to say about that, too. "I have a theory," he said, "that with youth there is a certain amount of ignorance that creates bliss. I felt more pressure winning one gold medal in 1968 at 22 than winning four at 18. The older one gets, the more complex life gets, and the tougher it is to maintain concentration."

Even the Ultimate American Boy grows up, ultimately.

OLYMPIC RESUME: *With wins in 1964 in the 100- and 400-meter freestyles as well as the 400- and 800-meter freestyle relays, Don Schollander became the first swimmer to win four golds at a single Games.*

SHE WAS ONE OF THE MOST proficient specimens ever produced by the German Democratic Republic's infamous sports machine. The authorities found her when she was six, swimming in a factory sports club in her hometown of Bitterfeld, a typically smoggy, smelly East German industrial city. They plucked her out of childhood and sent her to Halle to a full-time specialized training program. From then on Kornelia Ender saw her parents only on weekends. "I was a little dubious at the prospect," she recalled, "but I soon adapted." Six days a week the little girl arose at dawn, swam for two hours, went to class until noon, then spent the afternoon in a variety of training regimens, which included weightlifting, gymnastics, isometrics and more swimming—a total of six to eight miles every day. She said, "There were times when, honestly, I felt I'd had a snootful of training. But I never seriously thought of giving up."

Just 13 at the Munich Games in 1972, Ender was one of only three female swimmers from the G.D.R. to win individual medals—none of them gold. This was a typical showing for the East German women in those days—they had failed to win a single Olympic race since their nation became a sovereign state in 1949. All that changed in 1973, when the G.D.R. women swimmers burst on the scene as an instant powerhouse at the world championships in Belgrade. Led by Ender, still only 14, they won 10 of 14 events and broke seven world records. The women were big and seemed unnaturally muscular. "Oxlike" was a common, if cruel, description of Ender, who stood 5'11" and weighed 170 pounds. There were charges of steroid use from frustrated Americans, who for years had reigned over the sport. The G.D.R.'s head coach, Rudolf Schramme, denied the accusations, saying, "For years we learn from the Americans, and now they ask what our secret is."

When the East German women swimmers arrived in Montreal in 1976, there was much comment about their bulky musculature and deep voices. One G.D.R. coach responded, "We are here to swim, not to sing." And swim they did, winning 11 of 13 possible golds, with Ender taking four. Due to some bizarre scheduling, she raced twice in one 27-minute period and won gold twice—in the 100-meter butterfly and the 200-meter freestyle.

The main victim of this onslaught was Shirley Babashoff of the U.S., then 19. She had entered six events and ended up with one gold and four silvers—three of them in events won by Ender. Babashoff refused to congratulate the victors and was christened Surly Shirley by the press. But she was certain that steroids had robbed her of a once-in-a-lifetime opportunity to win five golds— and millions of dollars in endorsements.

Late in 1991, 20 former East German coaches signed a statement confessing that indeed they had fed their swimmers a steady diet of anabolic steroids during all those years of dominance. Babashoff, then 33 and a postal service employee in Southern California, was understandably angry. "It was a rip-off," she told *The Washington Times*. "I have never in my whole life seen girls who look like that. They were bigger than the guys swim team. I was in the locker room with them, and, like, I didn't want to change.... I've been dubbed a loser ever since then … just because I lost to a half-man, half-woman."

Kornelia Ender-Grummt, also 33, a physiotherapist living in southwest Germany with her husband and daughter, also replied to the revelations: "Now, after all this time, I still ask myself whether it could be possible they gave me things, because I remember being given injections during training and competition. But this was explained to me as being substances to help me regenerate and recuperate.... Medical men are the real guilty people. They know what they have done. When they gave us things to help us 'regenerate,' we were never asked if we wanted it, it was just given."

OLYMPIC RESUME: *At Munich in 1972, Kornelia Ender won the 100- and 200-meter freestyles, the 100-meter butterfly and the 400-meter medlay relay to become the first female swimmer to win four gold medals at a single Games.*

IN 1945, ROBERT KILLY, A native of Alsace and a World War II Spitfire pilot for the Free French, brought his family—a wife, a little girl of four and a little boy of two—from the environs of Paris to the village of Val d'Isère at the high end of the Tarentaise valley in the Savoie region of the French Alps. Upon arrival the Killys were dubbed "Chinese"—aliens—by the natives, and today, 47 years later, their status has not changed. Nevertheless, the village will likely never produce anyone more famous, more successful or more glamorous than the little outsider named Jean-Claude Killy, who grew up to win three gold medals at the age of 24 in France's Winter Olympics of 1968 in Grenoble, and then grew up even more to become at 48 the polished, ambassadorial copresident of France's Winter Olympics of 1992 in Albertville.

No matter that he was born near Paris, Killy quickly became a wild and wily mountain boy, a clever little truant who constantly skipped school and cut catechism to ski or hunt, and who finally dropped out of formal education altogether when he was 15 to concentrate on ski racing. His early races were performed in a state of perpetual free-fall. His coach, the brilliant Honoré Bonnet, recalled, "I took him on the team in 1960–61, and he never finished a race. He'd be ahead by two seconds halfway down, but he'd fall. I encouraged him. I told him that I selected people not by their finish but by their performance in the gates on the way down. I reminded him that, of course, if he wished ever to win, he would have to arrange to also finish."

Once Killy arranged to finish, he came in first with such regularity that he was all but invincible: During the 1966–67 season he won a phenomenal 23 of 30 races on the World Cup circuit, including all five downhills. In the summer of '67 Killy met a man who would change his life—Mark McCormack, the sports marketing guru from Cleveland. McCormack recalled his first dinner with Killy: "He ordered a glass of wine, and I made some crack about how he was breaking training. He sipped from his glass and said, 'Would you rather I drank milk and skied like an American?'" The Grenoble Olympics were on the horizon, but Killy asked McCormack a shocking question: "I had such a great season in '67, shouldn't I retire now? My value is very large, and what if I lose at Grenoble?" McCormack replied very quickly, "Whether you lose or win in the Olympics doesn't matter. The Games are so big that you will get publicity you can't get any other way."

Thus Killy was saved for Olympic posterity as well as for his own immense prosperity (in 1990 he estimated his fortune at about $20 million). His triple-gold performance at Grenoble was all daredevil tactics and hypertension. He won the downhill by an eye-blink of .08 of a second, made two headlong charges down the giant slalom course to win by a large margin, then suffered through a maddening and suspenseful five-hour judges' debate over whether or not his leading rival, Austria's Karl Schranz, had missed two gates in the pea soup fog that covered the slalom course.

From 1968 on, with McCormack's wise guidance, he became a global sex symbol, tabloid idol and television huckster of everything from Chevrolets to champagne. He also appeared in a dreadful 1972 film called *Snow Job*, a box-office disaster that persuaded him to put a stop to his acting career immediately.

In late 1981 he committed himself full-time—and unsalaried—to a grueling worldwide campaign to win the '92 Winter Games for Albertville. "There were 91 IOC members in 46 countries," he recalled. "I saw 50 people at home in 35 countries.... We knew nobody [at first]. Then we got to know them by their first names. Then we got to know their whole families by first names." In October 1986 the IOC gave the Games to Albertville. Not by coincidence, all but one of the men's Alpine ski racing events were located in Val d'Isère, where the natives had no choice but to agree that Jean-Claude Killy had done pretty well—for a Chinese.

OLYMPIC RESUME: *With victories in 1968 in the downhill, slalom and giant slalom, Jean-Claude Killy became one of only two men to win all three Alpine ski events at a single Games.*

BOB BEAMON

IT HAS BEEN TOUTED AS the greatest single athletic achievement of all time. If so, it certainly was all the greater for the fact that it was accomplished by an athlete who was convinced he had not the remotest chance of winning. Why? Because he had broken one of the hoariest cardinal rules in all of sport: *He had sex the night before a major competition!* In his biography of Bob Beamon, *The Perfect Jump*, Dick Schaap put it this way: "Beamon made love passionately, and when he burst into orgasm, just as the last trace of tension ebbed from his body, just at the best possible moment, he suddenly felt miserable.... *Oh my God,* thought Beamon, *I've ruined it.* I've left the gold medal right here. I've left the gold medal in the bed."

Now that moldy shibboleth is discredited forever thanks to Beamon's mighty long jump the next day—an impossible leap of 29' 2½", which was a full 21¾" beyond the existing world record. No one could believe it. The marker on the judges' optical measuring device fell off short of the point Beamon's feet had hit the sand, and the judges had to use a tape to measure the jump. The scoreboard flashed the official result at 8.90 meters. American track buffs in the stadium quickly began trying to convert meters to feet and inches—and found it maddening. They kept coming up with *29 feet* and something—clearly impossible. One coholder of the world record at the time, the magnificent Soviet Igor Ter-Ovanesyan, knew exactly how far Beamon had jumped. He turned to Lynn Davies, the Welsh jumper who had won the gold medal in 1964, and said quietly, "Compared to this jump, the rest of us are as children."

Beamon himself couldn't do the calculations either. When Ralph Boston, the other coholder of the world record, finally told him the incredible results, Beamon's legs gave way, and he fell, weeping, to the running track. At that same moment competitors in the 400-meter finals were lining up at their start, tense and eager to get under way before a coming thunderstorm struck. "Bob's jump held up our race for five or 10 minutes," recalled American sprinter Lee Evans. "He was on his knees in Lane 6 or 7,

sobbing, and Boston and Charlie Mays [another U.S. jumper] were trying to get him up. I wondered what the hell was going on." Despite the delay Evans ran that 400 in a mind-boggling 43.86 seconds, another legendary world record that stood for more than 20 years.

But Beamon's jump was almost beyond comprehension—in part because it occurred in an event that, for decades, had seemed to defy significant advancement. In 1901 an Irishman jumped 24' 11¾", and though he broke the record by just four inches, his mark stood for 20 years until an American upped it by a bare 3¼". In the next 14 years it went up by inches until Jesse Owens jumped 26' 8¼" in 1935. This was merely six inches more than the existing mark, but it lasted 25 years.

Many people predicted that Beamon's record would last forever. The unique combination of Mexico's thin air at high altitude and the fact that the maximum allowable wind of two meters per second had been blowing made his feat seem untouchable. Beamon himelf never came within two feet of his miracle mark; his best competitive outdoor jump after the Olympics was 26' 11" at the 1969 AAU national championships. In 1970 he didn't reach 26 feet all year, and in the national championships he couldn't break 23 feet and finished an abysmal 21st. Eventually he joined a professional track tour and competed sporadically until 1976, when he retired to go into youth work and coaching.

A crop of good jumpers had been inching up on the mark for years—particularly the American Carl Lewis, who had come closest at 28' 10¼". Then, on August 31, 1991, U.S. jumper Mike Powell flew 29' 4½" at the world championships in Tokyo. In interviews Beamon was gracious, almost matter-of-fact. Clearly he was aware that the immortal quality of his great leap remained unchanged. "Mine was a jump way before its time," he said. "It almost made it into the 21st century."

OLYMPIC RESUME: *Bob Beamon won the gold medal in the long jump at the Mexico City Games in 1968 with a world-record leap of 29' 2½", a mark that would stand for 23 years.*

DURING THE MID-1960S, before his Olympic fame, Kip Keino enrolled in a police academy on Kenya's northern border. During a patrol he found three children wandering alone, refugees from a conflict between the Kenyan government and Somali dissidents. "The children were starving," Keino recalled. "They were eating soil." He took them to the cottage he shared with his wife, Phyllis, a nurse, and the couple fed them, clothed them and sent them to school. The two girls grew up to have children of their own while the boy became a policeman in Karisa.

This was just the beginning: Over the next quarter century–plus Kip and Phyllis Keino took in more than 100 orphans. They lived most of that time on a 190-acre farm called Kazi Mingi in Kenya's western highlands, which Keino bought with the money he made following his four Olympic medals in 1968 and '72.

Keino was born sometime in January 1940 on a farm in Kapchemoiywo, a village of mud huts overlooking the Rift Valley about 240 miles northwest of Nairobi. His mother died when he was two, and he grew up in the hut of his maternal grandmother. He recalled that he was frequently beaten with a cane by a cruel uncle. "I suppose my upbringing contributed a bit to my outlook," he said. "Don't make others suffer." Nandi was his native language, but he learned rudimentary English at a Protestant missionary school, although he practically had to do it on the sly. He recalled, "My father did not like it when I went to school because then I could not watch the cattle."

At 18 he left his life of cattle-watching, entered the police academy and later became a sports instructor there. He also became a cross-country runner, and at 22 he was selected as a member of the Kenyan team that traveled to the Commonwealth Games in Perth, Australia—his first trip abroad. He did not make his first real international impression until 1964 at the Tokyo Olympics, where he finished fifth in the 5,000-meter run. By 1965 he had become a regular—and a crowd favorite—on the world track circuit. He brought an effortless stride and a unique effervescence to his races. Typically he wore a long-billed

cap of brilliant orange that he kept pulled down to his ears until he approached the finish, at which point he would fling it joyfully off his head and explode into his final sprint to victory. That first year on the tour he startled his rivals by setting world records in the 3,000 and the 5,000.

His rivalry with the great distance runners of the day—the U.S.'s Jim Ryun and Australia's Ron Clarke—attracted heavy press coverage. The three of them exchanged victories over the years, but both Ryun and Clarke were star-crossed when it came to the Olympics. Keino got the medals, while they both went home empty-handed. After Munich in 1972 Keino turned professional and profited nicely as one of the best-known runners on earth.

He continued to travel in the 1980s, appearing in Masters races and the like, but the Kazi Mingi farm and its shifting population of homeless children was the center of his world. In 1987 he was chosen as one of that year's SPORTS ILLUSTRATED Sportsmen of the Year for the generosity of his work. At that time he and Phyllis had 29 girls and six boys, aged one to 22, living at Kazi Mingi—plus their own seven children. Besides the farm Keino owned a sporting goods store, and even though the couple received some charitable donations, the shop was their major source of income. "We don't like to beg, beg, beg," said Phyllis. "If people donate, we don't object. But let them give when they are willing." Fortunately Kazi Mingi was its own source of sustenance: There were fruit trees, a large vegetable garden and 30 cows, which provided much-needed milk as well as dung to fuel the bio-gas energy system that lighted the house.

Over the years the occupants of Kazi Mingi came from many Kenyan and Ugandan tribes—the Boran, Kikuyu, Luo, Marakwet, Meru. "They're all my children," said Kip Keino. "I don't know any different."

OLYMPIC RESUME: *In 1968 Kip Keino won a gold medal in the 1,500 and a silver in the 5,000-meter run. In 1972 he won a gold in the 3,000-meter steeplechase and a silver in the 1,500-meter run.*

MARK SPITZ

IT DID NOT DAWN ON Olympic security experts until very late in the crisis that Mark Spitz, as a Jew and the reigning hero of the Munich Games, might make an irresistible target for the same Palestinian terrorists who had taken a group of Israeli Olympians hostage in the Olympic Village sometime before dawn on Sept. 5, 1972. At 9 a.m., roughly four hours after the siege began, Spitz walked out of his quarters in the Village—unguarded and completely ignorant of the desperate events

unfolding. He did not learn what was going on until later, at a press conference elsewhere in the Village. Only then did anyone think to tell Spitz that he might be in danger. "They'd just take me hostage—they wouldn't kill me, would they?" Spitz asked nervously. No one knew, but to be safe U.S. authorities posted five guards at his room and arranged to hustle him out of Munich 24 hours ahead of schedule. During a farewell press conference Spitz refused to stand at a battery of microphones, preferring to remain crouched within a protective huddle of U.S. team officials and uniformed guards. Reporters were upset because they could not hear his answers, and the conference ended in a storm of anger, most of it directed at Spitz.

Spitz seemed to have a knack for attracting anger in the wake of his seven gold medals in Munich. At one point he was asked if he found any irony in the fact that he was an all-conquering Jew in the country of the Holocaust. He shrugged and said, "Actually, I've always liked this country." Then he casually tapped a lampshade and added, "Even though this shade is probably made out of one of my aunts." He was relentless—and shameless—in his post-Olympic pursuit of cash. He once said coolly to an interviewer, "I'm a commodity, an endorser. It's like a game to see how much money I can make. It's just amazing to me. I thought maybe I'd make $20,000, enough to pay my way through dental school. But I guess I've caught on as a symbol or something. I know I'm lucky, but I also feel I'm entitled to make a buck." At a press conference someone asked him how many endorsement offers he had received, and he cracked, "How many clouds are in the sky?" The

Los Angeles Times suggested he was being merchandised as "a chunk of plastic livestock," and *The New York Times* dismissed him as "just another pretty face." But Spitz had the last laugh: His endorsement contracts alone were estimated at $5 million in the first year after Munich.

In 1973 he wed Suzy Weiner, a model, and they have been together ever since. "She stands on her own, and she's made me a nicer guy," said Spitz. Their son, Matt, was born in 1981, and the family settled into a four-bedroom house in Los Angeles. Spitz, no longer a "commodity," had a successful surfwear business as well as a prosperous home-building company and plenty of time and money to pursue his favorite hobbies—skiing and collecting art. "We've calmed down considerably," Suzy said. "We're not Hollywood types. We're family oriented."

Well, up to a point. In 1990, at the age of 40, Spitz announced that he planned to try to make the U.S. Olympic swimming team for the 1992 Barcelona Games in the 100-meter butterfly. Experts declared it a long shot at best, but Spitz, ever ready for a challenge, said with a touch of the old arrogance, "I am the Martian man come to life in sports. If you had to create a situation to test the body, here's a guy who was great. He has taken care of himself. He has been sort of hibernating, time warped. We'll see what happens."

What happened were a couple of heavily hyped made-for-TV races in April 1991 sponsored by Clairol Option, a men's hair color solution. The hirsute Spitz took on a couple of more recent U.S. Olympians, Tom Jager and Matt Biondi. Alas he lost both races by enormous—some thought embarrassing—margins. Still he kept on training until he was forced to face the sad and inevitable truth: The Martian man was an earthling after all.

OLYMPIC RESUME: *At the Munich Games in 1972, Mark Spitz won seven gold medals, more than any athlete has ever won in a single Olympic Games. The victories in all seven events came in world-record times.*

"IT IS A FACT THAT I HAVE the best singing voice on the Soviet weightlifting team," he said. "We sing often, songs of winning and songs of workers. We must struggle in competition, and we inspire ourselves by singing. Sometimes we sing about trenches and war, and sometimes about the Don flowing red with blood. Also a favorite of mine is *Yesterday* as Tom Jones sings it."

Vasily Alexeyev was recognized in the 1970s as the strongest man in the world—some said the strongest in history. He was a marvelously massive man, weighing 324 pounds at his best and standing 6' 1½", with an intimidating, operatic manner that was offset by sparkling dark eyes and a beatific smile that made wreaths of his great blue-bearded jowls.

At the height of his celebrity Alexeyev lived in the coal-mining city of Shakhty on the steppes about 800 miles southwest of Moscow. Officially his occupation was mining engineer, and he was paid a relatively high Soviet salary, 500 rubles (about $700) a month, although he never worked at it. "Being famous, as I have been," he said, "is not all positive. It makes it more difficult to go upward in your working career. Of course, I am not striving to go upward in my career at this moment. If I achieve too much as a mining engineer, it becomes more difficult to pursue my training as a sportsman. I also know that if I were working my way up in my mining-engineer career, I would be a big chief by now."

He and his family—two boys and a wife improbably named Olimpiada—lived then in a lovely brick bungalow that was built around 1913. It was owned by the state, and Alexeyev's rent was a token 12 rubles a month. The house and grounds were surrounded by a grapevine-festooned brick wall. Enclosed by the wall was a charming garden—the pride and joy of the strongest man in the world. "To make something in the earth, that is the best recreation yet," said Alexeyev. "I have three sorts of strawberries, and I have put them all together and made a new kind. My lovely Bulgarian peppers, there are none in Shakhty so crisp and pungent as mine. I have also made a

new sort of rose, so new they have no name, so I will name them Shakhtinka after the lovely women of Shakhty.... In my yard is perfect communism. I grow everything I need."

He built a billiard room in a small outbuilding behind his house as well as a garden gazebo with a Ping-Pong table in it. "I play often," he said. "I am best table tennis player on Soviet weightlifting team. I am also best on the team at draughts, dominoes, billiards and, of course, lifting the weights."

In his heyday he was one of the most popular heroes in the Soviet Union. "I am asked to make many speeches," he said. "I am very much at ease, and I say to crowds, 'O.K., what topic do you like me to talk about?' They ask me to tell how I got to be a great sportsman, and they ask my impression of my last competition. Of course, I have nearly always won the last competition, so my impressions are always happy, proud."

But happy and proud were hardly appropriate descriptions for Alexeyev after his appearance in the Moscow Olympics in 1980. He was 38 by then and, due possibly to injuries, had not been seen in international competition for two years. When it was his turn to compete before eager hometown fans in Moscow, he looked immensely overweight. Three times he tried to snatch 397 pounds, a weight he had bettered by 11 pounds in Montreal. Three times he failed. The Russian crowd jeered and whistled. He never competed again.

In 1990 Alexeyev, then 48, took over as head coach of the Soviet weightlifting team. His one major principle of training, he said, was that all illegal drugs were forbidden. Though steroids have long been a staple among champion weightlifters, and any team competing without them could be at a disadvantage, Alexeyev gave no quarter: "As long as I remain in this post, there can be no talk of doping."

OLYMPIC RESUME: *The first man to lift 500 pounds, weightlifter Vasily Alexeyev won gold medals in the superheavyweight division in 1972 and '76. He also won eight straight world championships and set 82 world records.*

BRUCE JENNER

HE MET HIS THIRD WIFE through baseball's man-about-the-boudoir Steve Garvey and Garvey's second wife, Candace. It began during a fishing trip in Alaska. Jenner recalled, "I was giving Candace a hard time about her perfectly coordinated outfit in the backwoods of Alaska, and she said, 'I've got this girlfriend you have to meet. She has a Ph.D. in shopping—great clothes, perfect taste!' I'm thinking, The last thing I need is a girl with a Ph.D. in shopping. Then Candace said, 'The only thing

is, she's got four kids.' I said, 'O.K., then, I'll go out with her because I have four kids, too.'" He was married to Kris Kardashian in April 1991 in a wedding that had four flower girls and four ring bearers—all children produced by the couple in three previous marriages.

Before he became world famous and rich as a result of his decathlon victory in Montreal in 1976, Bruce Jenner attended Graceland College, a small Mormon school in Lamoni, Iowa, on a football scholarship. There he met Chrystie Crownover, a minister's daughter. They were married in 1972, and she left school to work and support him so he could finish college. After the Olympics author Phillip Finch wrote a biography with Jenner in which he recited a favorite family joke: "If they should ever divorce, there may be a nasty argument over who gets custody of Bruce's diploma." More to the point, perhaps, was custody of Bruce's gold medal: Chrystie had also supported him while he trained for the decathlon in San Jose, California. After his ordeal performing the 10 events in Montreal, she wept copious tears and gave numerous interviews to the press about how difficult her sacrifices had been. In one of the interviews she confessed that she had sought psychiatric treatment "to become my own person, to like myself."

Before his victory Jenner said, "I do know that if I win and I handle myself well, I can work off it for years and years." He was worried that after winning he would be perceived as just another post-Olympic gold digger like Mark Spitz. He said, "I'm scared to say anything now. Everybody is ready to be reminded of Spitz. If I mention one thing about what I'm considering, everybody'll say,

'Hey, the kid's just in it for the money.'"

But money there was and plenty of it, including endorsement deals with Wheaties, Minolta, Tropicana and London Fog. By 1977 the Jenners had a house in Malibu, a $35,000 Porsche, three motorcycles and a $500,000-a-year income. They had a child in 1978. Bruce did on-camera work for NBC-TV's *Sportsworld*, made dozens of speeches at $5,000 per and appeared in a very bad movie called *Can't Stop the Music.*

Three years later he owned two Porsches, a Jeep, a Beechcraft Bonanza, two trail bikes, four Jet Skis, a Hobie 18 sailboat and some go-karts. "The difference between a man and a boy is the price of his toys," he said. "I worked hard for the Olympic medal, and now I can sit back and enjoy the rewards." Chrystie was pregnant with their second child, and they were about to be divorced. He said, "One of my problems was that I could never live up to, quote, Bruce Jenner, unquote. I mean, because of the Olympics, people put me up on such a high pedestal.... Bruce Jenner, all-American, apple pie and ice cream, and all of a sudden zappo! into a divorce. But it happens. I'm human, too."

After the breakup with Chrystie, he dated and later married Linda Thompson, Miss Tennessee of 1972, who was somewhat famous in her own right for having lived with Elvis Presley for five years and for being a regular on the syndicated TV show *Hee Haw.* He took up auto racing and played some regional theater, including a role in *Li'l Abner.* Linda bore two children, but in 1986 these Jenners were divorced, too. She told PEOPLE magazine, "We have a great relationship, but not a marriage."

At 41 he married again, this time to Kardashian. His endorsements and demands for personal appearances had dwindled. PEOPLE described him as "a professional car racer [who] ... also co-owns a business that enables people to store their blood for emergencies."

OLYMPIC RESUME: *Bruce Jenner won the decathlon at the Montreal Games in 1976 by one of the largest margins in Olympic history.*

PEGGY FLEMING WAS 12 IN 1961 when a plane carrying the entire U.S. figure skating team crashed in Brussels on the way to the world championships in Prague. Gone were all of America's world-class skaters, most of its promising young skaters and many of their coaches—73 people dead in all, including Fleming's coach Bill Kipp. Many experts believed it would be many years before the U.S. returned to power in the sport, but the child Fleming, forged in the crucible of disaster, as it were, stepped

into the void and helped to ease that catastrophic loss—at least a little.

"I didn't have anyone to look up to and guide my training," Fleming recalled, "but that was good in a way. To try to copy someone is never a good thing. Being the first of the skaters after the plane crash to do well definitely helped my career. There were a lot of special feelings when I won, feelings that I was more than just another champion, that I was the first to rise above the tragedy."

Her father was a newspaper printer of the old—meaning itinerant—breed, and the family had moved many times around the U.S. and Canada. Peggy first put on skates in the Cleveland Arena during a sojourn in that city. She was nine, and her older sister, Janice, recalled, "We had never been near an ice rink before, but we were looking for something to do. It was amazing. Peggy took to skates right off. She didn't wobble or anything, she just started skating as though she had been at it for a long time."

Peggy's talent was profound, and eventually the transient Flemings moved to Colorado Springs, near the Broadmoor Hotel skating school, so she could get first-class coaching. Carlo Fassi, a former Italian champion and coach who had been lured to the U.S. did some tinkering with her technique—but not much. "Peggy had style and natural feeling you don't teach," he said later. "She was the queen of skating, but she made it appear so easy and lovable, a lot of little girls fell in love with it." Dick Button described her this way: "She is a delicate lady on the ice. She is not a fiery skater, and she shouldn't be made to be. With some skaters there is a lot of fuss and feathers, but nothing is

happening. With Peggy there's no fuss and feathers, and a great deal is happening."

She won the first of five consecutive U.S. titles in 1964, when she was 15, then finished sixth at the Innsbruck Olympics. Stylish though she was at free skating, her strength lay in the paralyzingly boring skills of school figures—a pedantic event involving the precise tracing on ice of seemingly endless variations of the figure eight. At that time school figures counted for a full 60% of a skater's score. At the '68 Grenoble Games, Fleming spent two days under the fierce scrutiny of nine judges, slowly cutting intricate eights in the ice. When it was over she held a virtually insurmountable 77.2-point lead over the runner-up.

For her free skating routine she had six costumes to choose from—all designed and hand-sewn by her mother, Doris. She settled on a chartreuse chiffon, which her mother had picked out at Macy's in New York because it matched the color of the chartreuse liqueur that was bottled at a monastery near Grenoble. "I mean, because of those monks and all," recalled Mrs. Fleming, "it sort of hit me as soon as I walked into the fabrics department."

The costume hit everybody at the Stade de Glace in Grenoble, too, and the crowd applauded with abandon as Fleming performed to Tchaikovsky's *Pathétique*. Her performance was hardly *pathétique*, but it was certainly not one of her best. She faltered several times, and Fassi covered his eyes and groaned. When she finished, she burst into tears. But her huge lead in figures held up, and the gold was hers.

Fleming began skating in professional ice shows soon after Grenoble, married a dermatologist in 1970, had a son in 1977, did more ice shows off and on, quit in 1981, had another son in 1988, then returned in the spring of 1991, at 42, to perform in an ice show again. Her resemblance to the shining child of 30 years earlier was startling.

OLYMPIC RESUME: *Peggy Fleming won the gold medal in figure skating at the 1968 Olympics in Grenoble, becoming perhaps the most popular of America's many ice skating champions.*

IT WAS LAWSON ROBERTSON, the legendary U.S. Olympic track coach, who said in exasperation, "There are two kinds of runners: human beings and Scandinavians!" He spoke those words after the 1928 Games in Amsterdam, where Paavo Nurmi had won the gold in the 10,000-meter race and the silver in the 5,000 while another great Finn, Ville Ritola, won the gold in the 5,000 and the silver in the 10,000, and Edvin Wide, a Swede, took the bronze in both events.

The Scandinavian dominance of Olympic distance events extended back to 1912 and would continue for years after Robertson made his remark. Three Finns swept all three medals in the 10,000 and took the gold and silver in the 5,000 in 1936. And Scandinavian superiority reached yet another dramatic peak in 1972 and '76, when a gaunt, enigmatic Finn named Lasse Viren won the 5,000 and the 10,000 in *both* Munich and Montreal. By then Robertson was long gone to his reward, and it was probably just as well, for Viren might have been too much for him.

Viren was a country policeman by profession, but his scraggly beard gave him an ascetic, ethereal look, a little like a Nordic John the Baptist recently emerged from a frozen wilderness. Actually Viren emerged from the village of Myrskylä (pop. 2,300), which was 65 miles northeast of Helsinki. He was born there in 1949, the third generation of his family in Myrskylä, and he returned there to live after his Olympic feats. He didn't like the thought of living in a city. "If I am on my way somewhere and I meet a friend," he said, "I want to be able to stop and talk, to have a coffee. You can do that here. In the city it is all schedules." Of his police work, he said, "The work is varied. We cover four counties and have to do paperwork and detective work and take care of traffic accidents." He said there had never been a murder in Myrskylä and that there may have been one suicide, but he wasn't sure.

His mother recalled, "Lasse was always a peaceful boy. He was terribly shy. It was like milking a cow to get him to say anything. But everything he wanted to do, he wanted to do perfectly." He began running in his early teens,

and at 18 he quit trade school so he could do *that* perfectly.

A late starter, Viren won his first major race in 1969, but was very inconsistent. At the Munich Olympics he was a long shot because he had finished seventh and 17th in the 5,000 and 10,000 at the previous European championships. Nevertheless, his father, a farmer and truck driver, had premonitions of victory. "He saw Lasse in a dream the night before the 10,000 meters," Viren's mother recalled. "Lasse came to him and said, 'I am going to win.' Before the 5,000 his father spoke in his sleep. He said, 'Where can we find a plate big enough for both of the gold medals?'"

The 10,000 in Munich was one of the most dramatic in history: Near the halfway mark, Viren tripped and fell, causing another runner to tumble over him. Viren was down for perhaps three seconds, and when he rose, the leading pack of runners was 35 yards ahead of him. He regained his fluid pace, moved steadily ahead and not only won the race but also broke the world record by a full second. Injury, illness and mediocrity plagued him over the next several years, and it was assumed he would be an also-ran in Montreal in 1976. Then he surprised the world yet again, winning the 5,000 and 10,000 and finishing fifth in the marathon, an event he had never run before.

Instead of praising him for his recovery from a slump, many track experts accused him of blood doping, a procedure in which a portion of an athlete's blood is extracted, stored, then later reinjected to increase endurance by adding oxygen-carrying capacity to the system. Viren ridiculed the charges, and many of his rivals stood up for him. Frank Shorter, winner of the 1972 marathon, wrote in his autobiography, "There isn't a runner anywhere for whom I have greater respect than Lasse Viren. I do not believe he blood-doped.... In all four of his gold medal–winning races, he was simply the best man in the field."

OLYMPIC RESUME: *Lasse Viren achieved perhaps the most remarkable double double in history by winning the 5,000- and 10,000-meter runs in both 1972 and 1976.*

HE WAS BORN IN THE TINY village of Mooswald in the Austrian province of Carinthia near Yugoslavia, far from the famous ski areas. He once tried for several minutes to explain the location of Mooswald to a reporter, then gave up, concluding lamely, "It's just too far from anywhere." He spent his boyhood mowing hay and milking the family cows by hand, and when he attained early affluence as a World Cup skier, one of the first things he bought was a milking machine. Even after his great Olympic victory, when someone asked him what he was going to do, he replied, "My father already has the pitchfork waiting. We have to spread the dung for the spring planting."

Franz Klammer took up skiing at the age of 10, and from the moment he emerged from his world of cows and pitchforks, he displayed all the wildness and courage that eventually made him the "Austrian Astronaut"—the greatest downhill racer of them all. In December 1973, just 20 and starting his second season on the World Cup circuit, Klammer electrified skiing by rocketing down a course of boilerplate ice in Schladming at an astonishing average speed of 111.22 kilometers—69 miles—per hour. Not only was this his first World Cup victory, it also broke the all-time record for speed in a downhill race. Young and brash though he was, Klammer was awed by his feat: "I don't think anything beyond that can be demanded of a downhill racer. It was the limit of what can be done."

From then on, he skied very close to that limit. He won eight downhills out of nine during the next season, and from January 1976 through January 1977, he won 10 downhills in a row—including his victory at the Innsbruck Olympics, which some fans consider an individual performance in sport equivalent to Don Larsen's perfect game in the 1956 World Series. Certainly no athlete ever faced more pressure than Klammer, the homeboy, did on that day.

A crowd of 60,000 people carpeted the face of Patscherkofel mountain, and they began to roar the instant Klammer sprang out of the starting shack. He was No. 15, the last of the first seed, and all of his toughest rivals had already raced. Switzerland's Bernhard Russi was the leader with a time of 1:46.06. Klammer flung himself down the mountain, his skis clattering on the washboard ice, his arms flailing. At the halfway mark, he was clocked at .19 of a second behind Russi's time at the same spot, a large margin to overcome. As he burst into the last 1,000 meters, he forced himself to ski a reckless line. He nearly fell at one gate, wrenched himself back into control, then streaked down the final schuss through bedlam. The thunder of the crowd up and down the mountain told him he had won—by a scant .33 of a second.

After Innsbruck the Astronaut kept on soaring, winning every one of his next 10 races through January 1977. Then in February, his brother, Klaus, 18, a budding racer, suffered a horrible fall, leaving him permanently paralyzed from the waist down. Though it may have been a coincidence, Franz lost his touch, going winless in World Cup downhill competition for a stretch of nearly four years. He did not even qualify for the Austrian Olympic team in 1980. He denied that his brother's accident was to blame, but he was baffled by his own demise, admitting that he could not figure out "what I did before that made me fast and what I'm doing now that makes me so slow."

Then, suddenly, his form returned. He won a downhill in Val d'Isère in December 1981 and said, "It's as if I was blocked before, as if there was a wall in my mind. It disappeared." He was not the Klammer of old, but he kept skiing, and in 1983, at 29, he finished second in the final race of the season to capture the World Cup downhill title for the fifth time in his career. He made one last attempt, in 1984 in Sarajevo, to repeat his Olympic triumph but could manage only a 10th-place finish in the downhill. The Astronaut had come back to earth—for good.

OLYMPIC RESUME: *Franz Klammer, perhaps the greatest downhill racer of all time, won the gold medal in the Olympic downhill in 1976 at Innsbruck, in his native Austria.*

THE WAY BELA KAROLYI, HER first serious coach, tells the story, he used to scout kindergartens around Romania for gymnasts, and he spotted her and a friend doing acrobatics on the other side of a crowded schoolyard one day during recess in Onesti, her hometown. In her tiny five-year-old body, Karolyi glimpsed great talent, and he was about to go to her when the bell rang ending recess. All the children ran en masse into the school, and he lost sight of her in the confusion. Panicked, he hurried from classroom to classroom, shouting into each one, "Who loves gymnastics?" When he hit the right one, the answer came from Nadia Comaneci and her friend, "We! We!" From that moment on, it was only a matter of a few million somersaults: In 1971 at the age of nine she became Romania's junior champion; in 1973 at 11 she was national champion; in 1975 at 13 she became the youngest gymnast ever to win the European championship; and in 1976, at 14, she burst upon the Games in Montreal, becoming the first gymnast to receive a perfect 10.

Some of her revolutionary routines were so physically demanding that the gymnastic critic Josef Goehler wrote in *International Gymnast* magazine, "From a biomechanic viewpoint, this is hardly conceivable." Despite the reckless vitality of her performances, her brooding dark eyes, impassive pale face and short blunt answers to questions made her seem sad and enigmatic. Sportswriters were frustrated by her toughness, and they worked frantically to find something likable, something colorful, something *human* about her. Was Nadia always sad? "I can smile. But I don't care to." Did she ever cry? "No, I never cry. I have never cried." What did she think of her Soviet rival who had been the toast of Munich in 1972 but played second fiddle four years later in Montreal? "Olga Korbut is just another gymnast." What did she think of her perfect 10's? "If it was perfect, I deserved it."

She went home a tiny queen, but then a sinister Romanian fog swirled up and hid her from the world. At 15 she tried to commit suicide by drinking bleach. She has explained that she was burned out from too much training.

She went into a hospital for a couple of days, and later she said she was "glad" she had taken the poison—"glad because I didn't have to go to the gym for two days." She gained weight—at one point carrying 140 pounds, compared to 85 in Montreal. Despite these crises she appeared regularly in major competitions, including the Moscow Olympics, where she won two golds and a silver. In all, between 1976 and 1984, when she retired, she won 21 gold medals in the Olympics and in world championships.

She was a star in her homeland—*the* star, in fact. A Romanian expatriate said, "She is the most famous of all Romanians—probably not even Dracula is as famous." She was a favorite courtesan in the regime of the maniacal Communist dictator Nikolae Ceausescu and his murderous family—particularly Ceausescu's brutal son, Nicu, who was once her lover. She lived in an eight-room villa in Bucharest, and she drove a Dacia (a Romanian-made Renault) with a special license plate that gave her the status of a top party official with the right to park anywhere, to speed everywhere and to drink before driving.

She was a guest of honor at the Los Angeles Olympics in 1984, but Romanian secret police dogged her everywhere. Back home Nicu scolded her for enjoying herself in L.A. When she was invited to be an honored guest at the '88 Games in Seoul, the Ceausescus refused to let her go.

Comaneci finally rebelled. On Nov. 27, 1989, she and six other people drove from Bucharest to a lonely road 10 miles from the Hungarian border. "It was midnight when we started walking through mud and open countryside," she told the London *Mail on Sunday*. "We were stumbling. Often we crawled through water and ice." Six hours later they saw a spiked silhouette of barbed wire against the sky and crawled through the border fence. Four days later she arrived in New York, saying, "I like life. I want to have a free life."

OLYMPIC RESUME: *In 1976 Nadia Comaneci earned seven 10's—the first perfect scores ever recorded—en route to gold medals in the all-around, the uneven bars and the balance beam.*

HE WON HIS FIRST GOLD medal in Munich after knocking out three other heavyweights—including Duane Bobick, the American who had already been annointed the Great White Hope of the future—but when a promoter promised him $1 million if he would turn pro, Teófilo Stevenson replied loftily, "I will not trade the Cuban people for all the dollars in the world." These were words dear to the heart of Fidel Castro, the Cuban Communist dictator, and two weeks later he praised the boxer's refusal to succumb to the "traffickers of bodies and of souls" who ran professional boxing.

From then on Stevenson ranked as a local hero of such stature that he became one of only three men whom every Cuban referred to by their first names alone—Fidel, Ché and Teófilo. The government gave him a two-story house in Havana, two cars and a five-bedroom villa in Delicias, the north-coast sugar town of his boyhood.

In return Stevenson never waivered in his refusal to turn professional. In 1974 SPORTS ILLUSTRATED ran a headline—HE'D RATHER BE RED THAN RICH—over a story about still another U.S. fight promoter who had offered him $1 million if he would defect. Stevenson had again refused, saying, "What is a million dollars against eight million Cubans who love me?"

He won his second gold medal in Montreal with almost regal ease. He dispatched his first three opponents in a total of 7:22, then stalked a Romanian opponent around the ring for almost three full rounds before the man's handlers tossed in a towel to stop the fight with 25 seconds left. To no one's surprise the omnipresent promoter Don King was eager to sign Stevenson. But even he couldn't overcome the Cuban's deep-seated convictions. "Professional boxing treats a boxer like a commodity, to be bought, sold and discarded when he is no longer of use," Stevenson said. "I wouldn't exchange my piece of Cuba for all the money they could give me."

Another successful U.S. promoter, Bob Arum, proposed $1 million for Stevenson to fight Leon Spinks. That fell through, so Arum countered by offering $1 million for an exhibition between Stevenson and Muhammad Ali, with most of Stevenson's purse going to INDER, the Cuban national sports institute. That deal was nearly closed, but then the U.S. Treasury Department stepped in and ruled that it violated conditions of the American trade embargo against Cuba.

Stevenson won his third gold medal in Moscow at the grim Olympic mutation that was boycotted by most of the West. Stevenson was far from being the terrible terminator of past Games. As SPORTS ILLUSTRATED's Ron Fimrite wrote: "In four tedious bouts, two of which actually went the full three-round distance, the dour Cuban expended about as much energy as the ordinary Free World prizefighter does in conversation with Howard Cosell. And if Stevenson established anything, it is that his own once-formidable gifts are on the decline. Either that or he is simply bored with the bum-of-the-month quadrennial campaign his amateur status has imposed on him."

After Moscow his performances were listless and uneven until early 1984 when surprisingly he seemed to be approaching his best form again. Did this mean he would go for a fourth gold in Los Angeles? Certainly not. The socialist world was boycotting those Games and Teófilo Stevenson, the model socialist, stayed home.

His job as a boxing adviser with INDER never paid him more than $400 a month. Yet he never showed a trace of regret that he had passed up millions. He told *The Washington Post* in 1989: "There are world champions who earn a lot of money, but they don't even know how to sign their names. They are not useful to their society. At the end of their careers, after earning so much money, they are in the same condition they began: without a penny. And they are even worse because they have burnt all their youth and they don't even know how to educate their own children. I have what I need. I feel happy inside."

OLYMPIC RESUME: *With victories in 1972, '76 and '80, heavyweight boxer Teófilo Stevenson became the only man to win three consecutive gold medals in the same weight division.*

HE WAS BORN THE SON OF A supermarket manager named Cicero and a nurse named Gertha. He was named Ray Charles Leonard after the blind singer, and he spent much of his youth in the predominantly black Baltimore suburb of Palmer Park. He was more interested in the church choir than anything else until he was 14. Then he discovered boxing and dubbed himself Sugar Ray after the great middleweight.

Going into the Olympics in Montreal he had won 145 of 150 amateur fights, three Golden Gloves titles, five international championships, two AAU crowns and a gold medal at the Pan Am Games. The U.S. team was considered inferior to the Cubans and the Eastern Europeans, but Leonard scoffed, "They are all computerized fighters. Especially the Russians. You don't have to wind them up because they come with lifetime batteries. You just push a button and away they go."

American boxers wound up dominating everyone, winning 35 of 41 fights for five gold medals, a silver and a bronze. A great favorite of the press, Leonard fought with painfully injured hands. After the Games he told an adoring world, "My journey has ended, my dream is fulfilled. Now I want to go to school. I have been an example for the young people as a fighter. Now I want to show them that you can be a champion at school, too."

But Leonard turned pro instead. Someone asked why he reneged on his promise to quit boxing. He said, "I guess you could say it was reality. My responsibilities." His mother had suffered a mild heart attack and could no longer work. His father was hospitalized with meningitis and tuberculosis of the spine. He had a son, Ray Charles Leonard Jr., born two years before the Olympics to his girlfriend—and later wife—Juanita Wilkinson. "They are down, and I am capable of lifting them up and putting them in a good financial position," he said.

His manager, the cagey Angelo Dundee, had picked for Leonard's first professional opponent a low-slung brawler named Luis (the Bull) Vega, who had a 14-8-3 record and agreed to fight for $650. Leonard's take was $40,044. Three years, 25 professional victories and almost $21 million later, Leonard held the WBC welterweight championship. He had bought his parents a $65,000 split-level house in suburban Maryland. His mother was well, and his father was back at work. Ray, Juanita and Ray Jr. lived on a six-acre, $750,000 spread, also in Maryland. Again, someone asked Ray why he was still fighting now that he was rich, and he said, "Fame comes and goes. I'm trying to get everything while I'm hot."

He lost the title in 1980 in an epic fight with Roberto Duran, then won it back in an infamous rematch five months later when Duran quit in the eighth round. Before that victorious fight, in a nice twist of history, his famous namesake, Ray Charles, sang *America the Beautiful*. The following year Leonard won a TKO over the previously unbeaten Thomas (Hit Man) Hearns in a marvelous bout. In 1982 he retired because of a detached retina. But still not for good. He came back in 1984, retired again, then returned to the ring again in 1987 and dazzled the world by defeating the hard-hitting Marvin Hagler. Leonard was ecstatic. "I went against history, and now they'll have to rewrite the books. Someone said before the fight, 'Two things will not happen this year: Oliver North will not be back in the White House, and Sugar Ray Leonard will not beat Marvin Hagler.' I think they better check the White House."

And still, he didn't quit. Finally in February 1991 at the age of 34, he suffered a humiliating defeat at the hands of Terry Norris, 23. For the fourth time since the 1976 Olympics, Sugar Ray Leonard retired. A month later it was revealed that while his career was on hold due to the detached retina, he had drunk heavily, used cocaine and abused his wife. He held a press conference, confessed his sins and said, "Here is a young man that had everything in the world, from money to fame, glory, a beautiful family. Why would he do that? It's almost inconceivable."

OLYMPIC RESUME: *Sugar Ray Leonard became the Olympic boxing champion in the light welterweight division in 1976, defeating Andrés Aldama of Cuba in the gold-medal match.*

1980-1992

THE COM
GAMES

MERCIAL

THE TWO OLYMPICS OF 1980 COULD NOT HAVE BEEN HELD IN MORE NIGHTMARISH SETTINGS. THE WINTER GAMES OCCURRED IN THE SMALL-MINDED, SNAFU-RIDDEN VILLAGE OF LAKE PLACID, NEW YORK, AND THE SUMMER GAMES TOOK PLACE IN THE HOOLIGAN-INFESTED, BOYCOTT-SHOT METROPOLIS OF MOSCOW. THESE WERE BAD DREAMS OF ENTIRELY DIFFERENT KINDS, BUT WHEN THEY WERE

THE DUO BEHIND THE SAVVY—SOME THOUGHT UNSEEMLY—
MARKETING OF THE GAMES: L.A. BOSS PETER UEBERROTH (RIGHT)
AND IOC PRESIDENT JUAN ANTONIO SAMARANCH

M O S C O W
1 9 8 0

SEBASTIAN COE
OUTKICKED COUNTRYMAN
STEVE OVETT (279) IN
THE 1,500-METER RUN TO
ACHIEVE SWEET
REVENGE FOR HIS
DISAPPOINTING LOSS TO
OVETT IN THE 800
SIX DAYS EARLIER

DRAMATICS ABOUNDED ON THE ICE, WHERE IRINA RODNINA AND ALEKSANDR ZAITSEV (ABOVE) WON THEIR SECOND STRAIGHT OLYMPIC PAIRS COMPETITION; ERIC HEIDEN WON AT EVERY SPEED SKATING DISTANCE TO BECOME THE FIRST ATHLETE TO COLLECT FIVE INDIVIDUAL GOLDS; AND THE U.S. HOCKEY TEAM (FAR RIGHT) UPSET THE MIGHTY SOVIETS 4–3 ON ITS WAY TO A SURPRISING GOLD MEDAL

BENCHMARKS

MARCH
Archbishop Oscar Romero is assassinated while conducting mass in El Salvador.

APRIL
The U.S. mission to rescue the hostages in Iran fails miserably.

APRIL
Alfred Hitchcock dies at 80.

MAY
Mount St. Helens erupts, killing eight people and sending up a 60,000-foot tower of ash.

AUGUST
Unions are legalized in Poland. Solidarity is formed one month later.

NOVEMBER
Ronald Reagan becomes president after defeating Jimmy Carter in a landslide.

DECEMBER
John Lennon is killed by a crazed fan.

1984

LOS ANGELES
SARAJEVO

ALL THE TENSION OVER DISRUPTIVE POLITICS

SEEMED TO DISSIPATE LIKE MORNING DEW IN THE WARM CALIFORNIA SUN

AS THE OLYMPICS MADE A PROFIT IN LOS ANGELES AND THE

GAMES ENTERED A SHINY NEW ERA OF CORPORATE SPONSORSHIP AND

HIGH-POWERED GLOBAL MARKETING

MARY DECKER WAILED IN PAIN AFTER A COLLISION WITH
ZOLA BUDD KNOCKED HER OUT OF THE 3,000-METER RUN;
EDWIN MOSES (RIGHT) CONTINUED HIS AMAZING STREAK: HIS
WIN IN THE 400-METER HURDLES WAS HIS 105TH STRAIGHT

LOS ANGELES **1984**

L.A. STORIES: MARY LOU RETTON (ABOVE)
WON THE ALL-AROUND FOR THE FIRST-EVER U.S. MEDAL IN
GYMNASTICS; MOROCCO'S SAID AOUITA TRIUMPHED
IN OLYMPIC-RECORD TIME IN THE 5,000; AND CARL LEWIS
STREAKED TO FOUR GOLD MEDALS, ONE OF THEM FOR
ANCHORING THE U.S. 4 X 100-METER RELAY TEAM (RIGHT)

EMOTIONAL PERFORMANCES OF VERY DIFFERENT SORTS
WERE PROVIDED BY FIERY U.S. SKIER BILL JOHNSON (RIGHT),
WHOSE FULL-THROTTLE CHARGE GAINED HIM THE
DOWNHILL GOLD, AND LYRICAL ICE ARTISTS JAYNE TORVILL
AND CHRISTOPHER DEAN OF GREAT BRITAIN, WHOSE
GOLD MEDAL PROGRAM IN ICE DANCING FINISHED
ON A DECIDEDLY DOWN NOTE

1988

SEOUL
CALGARY

A RESPITE IN CALGARY COULDN'T ASSUAGE FEARS OF

TERRORISM IN SOUTH KOREA, BUT BY THE END OF THE SUMMER GAMES A

DIFFERENT KIND OF CONTROVERSY HAD GRABBED THE

HEADLINES AS PERFORMANCE-ENHANCING DRUGS BESMIRCHED THE

INTEGRITY OF THE COMPETITION ITSELF

GREG LOUGANIS WAS SIMPLY THE FINEST DIVER EVER,
REPRISING HIS '84 VICTORIES IN THE PLATFORM AND
SPRINGBOARD EVENTS; JACKIE JOYNER-KERSEE DEMOLISHED
THE HEPTATHLON FIELD, THEN WON THE LONG JUMP (RIGHT)

OLYMPIC AUDIENCES WERE WOWED BY MATTI NYKÄNEN (ABOVE), WHO GAVE NEW MEANING TO THE TERM FLYING FINN WITH HIS RECKLESS SKI JUMPS THAT PRODUCED GOLD MEDALS ON THE 70- AND 90-METER HILLS; AND BY THE VIRTUOSITY OF DOWNHILL GOLD MEDALIST PIRMIN ZURBRIGGEN (FAR RIGHT) OF SWITZERLAND; BUT THE GLITTERING STAR OF THE GAMES WAS KATARINA WITT, THE GLAMOROUS DIVA FROM EAST GERMANY, WHO CAPTURED THE FIGURE SKATING GOLD FOR THE SECOND STRAIGHT TIME

CALGARY
1988

BENCHMARKS

FEBRUARY
General Manuel Noriega of Panama is indicted in Miami for illegal drug trafficking.

MARCH
John Poindexter and Oliver North are indicted in connection with the Iran-Contra affair.

APRIL
The Soviet Union agrees to withdraw from Afghanistan.

APRIL
TV evangelist Jimmy Swaggart is defrocked as a minister of the Assemblies of God.

NOVEMBER
George Bush is elected president.

DECEMBER
A bomb aboard a Pan-Am flight explodes over Lockerbie, Scotland, killing all 259 passengers and crew as well as 11 people on the ground.

1992

BARCELONA
ALBERTVILLE

FOR TWO GLORIOUS WEEKS IN FEBRUARY THE

CITY OF ALBERTVILLE, FRANCE, GAVE THE WORLD A CHARMING,

CONTROVERSY-FREE OLYMPICS THAT FEATURED A DIVERSE

COLLECTION OF INTERNATIONAL STARS. FIVE MONTHS LATER, BARCELONA

PROVED THAT THE NEW SPIRIT OF AMITY WAS NO FLUKE.

RAY LEBLANC'S HEROICS IN THE NET WEREN'T
ENOUGH TO GAIN A MEDAL FOR THE U.S. HOCKEY TEAM;
BONNIE BLAIR (RIGHT) GLIDED TO GOLD IN
THE 500- AND 1,000-METER SPEED SKATING EVENTS

CARL LEWIS RAN A LIGHTNING LAST LEG (LEFT) TO WIN HIS
EIGHTH GOLD MEDAL AND ANCHOR THE U.S. TO
VICTORY AND A WORLD MARK OF 37.40 IN THE 4X100-
METER RELAY; U.S DREAM TEAMERS (FROM TOP) LARRY BIRD,
MICHAEL JORDAN, SCOTTIE PIPPEN AND MAGIC JOHNSON
CRUISED TO GOLD AS WELL, BEATING THE OPPOSITION BY AN
AVERAGE MARGIN OF NEARLY 44 POINTS.

BARCELONA **1992**

A HAPPY SURPRISE FOR THE U.S. WAS THE PERFORMANCE
OF MARK LENZI, WHO WON THE SPRINGBOARD DIVING
EVENT, BECOMING THE ONLY NON-CHINESE PERFORMER—
MALE OR FEMALE—TO COME HOME WITH A GOLD
MEDAL IN DIVING.

KARL MALDEN, THE ACTOR who played coach Herb Brooks in the TV-movie *Miracle on Ice,* studied him on videotape and said, "I'd hate to meet him in a dark alley. I think he's a little on the neurotic side. Maybe more than a little. Any moment you think he's going to jump out of his skin."

Brooks's players had good reason to agree with that diagnosis. The coach was a cold-eyed perfectionist who seemed to believe that fear and loathing were the greatest motivators known to

man. He screamed at his players' mistakes and demanded obedience to his every order. He even devised a 300-question psychological test to help select his final team. As SPORTS ILLUSTRATED's E.M. Swift reported: "One player—an eventual Olympic hero—said, 'Herb, I'm not taking this. I don't believe in that stuff.'

"'Why's that?' Brooks asked.

"'Oh, it's a lot of bull, psychology.... I don't want to take it.'

"Brooks nodded. 'O.K. Fine. You just took it. You told me everything I wanted to know.' He was steaming.

"'How'd I do?'

"'You flunked.'

"The next day the player took the test."

Brooks loved the torture-training of wind sprints, sending his players up and down the rink until they were exhausted, then ordering them to do more. And more. And *more.* The sprints became known as Herbies, and even though such exercises were common, Brooks ordered far more of them than any other hockey coach would. One night during a training game in Norway in September 1979, the team played poorly and Brooks was enraged. Afterward he sent them onto the ice to skate Herbies as the crowd was leaving the arena. Soon the place was empty except for the maintenance crew. The Herbies went on. Bored and tired, the rink workers turned off the lights. Incredibly the Herbies went on in the dark. And on and on....

The torture had its purpose. It was Brooks's way of whipping his team into the same superhuman physical condition that had propelled the Soviets to four straight

Olympic gold medals. Though Brooks's players averaged just 22 years old and came from cushy American homes, they went to the Olympics in as good shape as any Soviet veteran. In the seven games in Lake Placid, the U.S. team was outscored 9–6 in the first period, but outscored its opponents 27–6 in the second and third.

They tied the tough Swedish team in the last 27 seconds, blew over the even tougher Czechoslovakian team by a 7–3 score, then defeated Norway, Romania and West Germany—each game remaining close until the last period, when the Herbies kicked in. The Soviet team played against them like the polished juggernaut it was, and the Americans fell behind three times before they tied the game at 3–3 in the third period. Then, with 10 minutes left in the game, captain Mike Eruzione scored what his teammate John Harrington labeled "one of the great slop goals of all time." Somehow the American boys kept the Soviet men at bay to the end, and then the world was treated to one of the great kid victory scenes of all time. Hugs, tears, rolling like puppies on the ice.

Later, back in the locker room, the enormity of their accomplishment swept over them. As Swift wrote: "It was then that somebody started a chorus of *God Bless America,* 20 sweaty guys in hockey uniforms chanting '... from the mountains, to the valleys, na-na-na-na-na-na-na-na....' Nobody knew the words. And where was Brooks? Holed up in the men's room, afraid to come in and ruin their celebration. 'I almost started to cry,' he says. 'It was probably the most emotional moment I'd ever seen. Finally I snuck out into the hall, and the state troopers were all standing there crying. Now where do you go?'"

One place the team had to go was back on the ice two days later to beat Finland. Had they lost, the U.S. would have finished *fourth.* But these children, egged on by their wicked old coach, won 4–2, and another Olympic fairy tale went into the books.

OLYMPIC RESUME: *The gold medal won by the U.S. hockey team in 1980 represented one of the greatest upsets in sports history.*

FLORENCE GRIFFITH JOYNER &
JACKIE JOYNER-KERSEE

LOADED WITH STEROIDS, BEN Johnson disgraced himself in Seoul, but he also cast a dark shadow over the brilliant performances of others in the Games—particularly those of the sisters-in-law who won or shared in five of the six gold medals won by the U.S. women's track team. Every press conference was filled with ugly questions about their muscular physiques. Jackie replied, "I'm not using drugs, I'm not on steroids.... I've read and heard that I've been described as an ape. I never thought I was the pret-

tiest person in the world. But I know that, inside, I'm beautiful.... Hey, it's sad for me. I worked hard to get here." The glamorous Flo-Jo adamantly denied the drug rumors, too.

Ironically, Flo-Jo and her husband, Al Joyner, Jackie's brother, had asked Ben Johnson in 1987 after he ran the 100 in 9.83 seconds exactly what he did to improve so dramatically over the previous two track seasons. Johnson said it was due to an extensive weightlifting program. Al said later, "We believed it when Ben told us how he lifted weights. We did it, believed in it, and it worked."

Flo-Jo and Jackie were phenomenal athletes, loving friends and profoundly different people. Florence Delorez Griffith grew up in the projects of Los Angeles with a mother who was a seamstress and a grandmother who was a beautician. "I learned crocheting, knitting, hair and nails," she recalled. She also learned a madly eccentric approach to life. At one point she owned a five-foot boa constrictor. "I bathed her and lotioned her. When she shed I saved all of her skin and painted it different colors." This, of course, was the same madcap sense of fashion that led her to invent the one-legged bodysuit and the lace running suit she called "an athletic negligee."

She had been a very good sprinter and long jumper in high school, and when she went to Cal State–Northridge she met a young sprint coach named Bobby Kersee. When he transferred to UCLA, she went, too. In 1982 she was the NCAA champion in the 200, and two years later she won the silver in Los Angeles. She quit serious training to be a bank secretary for a couple of years, then started again, and at the 1987 world championships she won a

silver medal in the 200 meters and a gold with the 4 x 100 relay team.

She had always been very, very good, but not a superstar. That changed suddenly in 1988. At the U.S. Olympic trials in Indianapolis she ran the 100 in 10.49 to crack Evelyn Ashford's world record of 10.76 by an unbelievable margin. According to expert projections, no woman was supposed to reach even 10.65 before the year 2000. Not only had she broken Ashford's record, she had done it in each of four different heats—and wearing four different costumes. Clearly, here was a star that had been waiting to be born.

In contrast to the flittering glitter of Flo-Jo, Jackie Joyner-Kersee symbolized what great talent, hard work and a good soul can do for you. Born in the forsaken town of East St. Louis, Illinois, in 1962, she was named after the then president's wife. Her grandmother said at her birth, "Someday this girl will be the first lady of something." As a child it seemed she would only be the first lady of poverty. Her brother Al said, "I remember Jackie and me crying together in a back room in that house, swearing that someday we were going to make it. Make it out."

They made it out in glorious style. He won the triple jump in L.A.—the first American in 80 years to do so in an Olympics—then married the dazzling Flo-Jo in 1987 and became her moral support and mentor when he didn't make the '88 Olympic team.

Jackie went to UCLA in 1980 on an athletic scholarship, played basketball and specialized in the long jump—until Bobby Kersee happened into her life. He saw the brilliant versatility of her athletic talent and began to train her for the heptathlon. "By 1982 I could see she'd be the world-record holder," he said later. On Jan. 11, 1986, coach and world-record holder became husband and wife in a tiny Baptist church in Long Beach, California. "This," promised the preacher, "is going to be a happy marriage."

OLYMPIC RESUME: *Sisters-in-law Florence Griffith Joyner (100-, 200-meter dash, 4 x 100-meter relay) and Jackie Joyner-Kersee (long jump and heptathlon) combined for five gold medals in 1988.*

IN 1980, A FEW MONTHS after his historic five-gold-medal spree, Eric Heiden said plaintively: "People ask me to give speeches, but I'm only 21 years old. What can I tell anybody?"

By simply realizing that, he proved himself smarter than a whole lot of older Olympic heroes. However, he might have let the world in on how he was able to accomplish what he did at Lake Placid, because no one else—least of all the experts in speed skating—could figure it out. Heiden finished first in every

race from the 500-meter sprint to the 10,000-meter quasi-marathon. The first victory took 38.03 seconds, the last nearly 15 minutes. Bill Rodgers, the U.S. marathoner, said as Heiden's medals piled up, "What Heiden is doing is comparable to a guy winning everything from the 400 meters to the 10,000 meters in track. My god! Equating it to running, it is doing the impossible!" Annie Henning, a gold medalist at the Sapporo Games in '72, was over-whelmed, too: "I don't believe what I am seeing when I see Eric skate. If he happens to misjudge a little and runs down, he always has another little muscle somewhere in that big body where he can pull out whatever power he needs. He's as close to perfect as you can get."

Not only did Heiden win all five races at Lake Placid, but he also broke five Olympic records and one world record. One of his rivals, Frode Rönning of Norway, said grimly, "It's not exciting to be skating now. The medals are delivered before the race." Rönning's coach, Sten Stenson, threw up his hands, too: "In Norway we say that if you can be good in the 5,000 and 10,000, you cannot do the 500. But Eric can do it. We have no idea how to train to take him. We just hope he retires."

Heiden alone won more gold medals than any U.S. team at the Winter Olympics since 1932, when Americans got six. He was the toast of the nation, which devoured all sorts of details about him—including the fact that when Levi's was outfitting the U.S. team for opening ceremonies, the only pair of pants that would fit over Heiden's 29-inch thighs had a 38-inch waist—six inches larger than his own.

Yet, through it all, the person least impressed with what he had done seemed to be Eric Heiden himself. He took to calling all the hype "The Great Whoopee"—a term he had borrowed from John Aristotle Phillips, who had given that name to the grand media fuss that arose a few years earlier when he revealed that he had designed a homemade atomic bomb while an under-graduate at Princeton. At one point, blinking into camera flashes and TV lights, Heiden sighed and said, "The Great Whoopee, it's kind of a drag."

He retired that same year, and the end of his skating career was not traumatic: It simply led to another chapter in his life. "I like my privacy," he said. "I don't like to see athletes hanging onto their past. You've got to move on." He moved on to a premed course at Stanford and turned down numerous lucrative offers to appear in films or on television—with one exception being appearances as a commentator for later Olympic telecasts. At the Sarajevo Games he was asked where he kept his gold medals. "I think they're under a bunch of sweaters," he said. However-er, he did know where his famed skintight golden racing suit was—in the Smithsonian Institution. "I thought that was pretty cool when they asked for it," he said.

He didn't forsake athletics entirely after Lake Placid, though. In 1985 he won a professional cycling champi-onship in the U.S., and in 1986 he raced in the grueling Tour de France. But he was never a cycling star and soon his energies were fully occupied by his studies at the Stan-ford medical school. He graduated in May 1991 and the following month began his internship in orthopedic surgery at the not-so-tender age of 33. "Ever since I was a little kid, I wanted to be a doctor," he said happily. "But I had to put it on the back burner. You can only use that athletic talent when you're young."

Certainly no one used it better—or knew better when to stop.

OLYMPIC RESUME: *With victories at every speed skating distance from 500 to 10,000 meters, Eric Heiden became the first athlete to win five individual gold medals at the Olympic Games.*

IT WAS THE FIRST MARATHON ever run by women in an Olympics, and she ran the third-best time ever produced by a woman—2:24:52. This was impressive by itself, but if we put it into historical perspective, it was mind-boggling: With that time, she would have won the gold medal in 13 of the 20 Olympic marathons run by men before her. Her time was 33:58 better than Spiridon Louis's dramatic triumph in 1896, 7:44 better than Hannes Kolehmainen's Olympic best and just 1:49 slower than Emil

Zátopek's. We might assume that this says more about the wonders of nutrition, training technology and general all-around health in the late 20th century than it does about Joan Benoit Samuelson herself. But, in fact, her victory in Los Angeles was of such a magnitude that to generalize about it at all is to deny one of the most inspiring individual triumphs in Olympic history.

Two and a half weeks before the Olympic trials in May '84, she underwent arthroscopic surgery on her right knee, which had suddenly begun to throb with piercing pain during a training run and then seized up so tightly that she couldn't complete a full running motion. Using microscissors in a tiny incision, Dr. Stan James of Eugene, Oregon, snipped a tight bundle of inflamed tissue from behind the joint on the outside of the knee. "You could hear it snap," he said. "It was like cutting a rubber band." The next day an exercise cycle was installed over her hospital bed, and she began pedaling with her hands to keep her cardiovascular system functioning at the same high level it had attained after months of intensive training. Two days after surgery she was exercising on a treadmill. Four days afterward she was running again—only a mile at first. Then she began to swim, ride a bicycle, lift weights—and finally return to long-distance runs. On May 12, exactly 17 days after surgery, she ran to qualify for the Olympics. Miraculously she won the trial; she wept as she crossed the finish line. How was this possible? Her coach, Bob Sevene, answered: "Joan has this tremendous ability to blank out everything at the start of a race—heat, humidity, injury or pain. It's the pure marathoner in her."

Few were ever purer. In April 1979, on the way to her first Boston Marathon, she got caught in traffic in a friend's car, jumped out in frustration and ran two miles to the starting line. A neophyte then, she was buried deep in the crowd of runners at the starting line but still finished first among women, in 2:35:15, then a Boston record. She seemed always to be overcoming an injury. In December 1981 she had surgery on both heels, was in casts for a month and couldn't train seriously for 10 weeks. Yet in September 1982 she won a marathon in Eugene, in 2:26:11, just 42 seconds shy of the world record. And seven months later she came back to win the Boston Marathon again, this time in 2:22:43, the best a woman had ever done—by a full two minutes and 47 seconds.

After winning the Olympic gold medal in Los Angeles, she married Scott Samuelson, and in 1987 she gave birth to their first child, Abigail. Soon after that she began to suffer chronic lower-back pain, and in Boston in 1989 she limped home a disappointing ninth. It seemed as if her career was coming to a close. She had a second child, Andre, in 1990. When she turned up at the start in Boston in 1991, she was 33 years old, her hair was flecked with gray, and she had stopped nursing Andre only a month before. She was unusually grim: "I'm not looking beyond this race. For me to continue, it's necessary to run under 2:30." She was still plagued by back pain. "I'm learning to work with it," she said. "I make the best of what I have."

Truer words were never spoken. To the astonishment of everyone, perhaps including herself, Benoit Samuelson ran the race in 2:26:54, good enough for a close fourth place. "I knew I'd be back as soon as I got over those medical problems," she said. "All I had to do was to get my head in the thick of things." It is worth noting that her head was one of the few parts of Joan Benoit Samuleson's body that had never let her down.

OLYMPIC RESUME: *Joan Benoit Samuelson won the first Olympic marathon for women, in Los Angeles in 1984.*

HE SEEMED ALWAYS TO BE conflicted about his public persona, one minute playing the imperious superstar, the next the modest and unassuming jock next door.

Before he was to run the anchor leg in the 4 x 100-meter relay in Los Angeles, someone asked him a dumb question, "What if you drop the baton?" Lewis replied sharply, "I pick it up and we win anyway." After the victory someone asked how he felt about replacing Jesse Owens in the hearts of Americans. "Hey," he said, "my job is just to compete as an athlete and be a nice guy. Jesse Owens is still the same to me, a legend. I'm just a person with some God-given talent."

Before the 1984 Games he had sat by quietly while his manager boasted to the press, "We think Carl will be bigger than Michael Jackson." He wasn't, in large part because people were put off by his prima donna ways—particularly his insistence on taking only as many long jumps as he needed to win and refusing to attempt more in a try for the world record. Four months after the Games, Lewis had signed exactly one endorsement deal, with a Japanese soft drink company, but he said, "I have no regrets.... Many tried to rip me, break me down over money, over being gay.... [But] I have so many fans."

He had his nose altered, took acting and singing lessons and predicted that in five years he would be "a respected entertainer and very happy." But he kept on competing and during the Seoul Olympics wound up with the gold medal in the 100-meter dash after Ben Johnson's disqualification for using steroids. Lewis was gracious in a difficult situation. "I feel very sad for Ben and for the Canadian public. You can talk track up to a certain point. After that you talk people. Imagine the burden on Ben. Imagine what his family will go through." At that point, SPORTS ILLUSTRATED's Kenny Moore wrote: "It's time to reexamine our perceptions of Lewis. When these bewildering Olympics recede enough to allow us a sense of proportion, we may not remember Johnson being found out as much as Lewis being revealed as the gentleman he has always been."

Still, Lewis remained obsessed with his public image. In *Inside Track*, his 1990 autobiography, he reported that after his pal Joe DeLoach beat him in the 200-meter final in Seoul, he advised DeLoach on how to run a victory lap: "Make sure you keep waving. Always give smiles. If you see somebody you know, give an extra little stare because people notice that. They think that's nice."

But the man was much more than imagery. At the 1991 world championships in Tokyo—with a brilliant 11-year career behind him that had already produced six Olympic golds and five world championship wins—he performed two feats that, by themselves, guaranteed his immortality, if not his lovability. First, in a 100-meter dash that may have been the best ever run, he burst through to a world record of 9.86 seconds. Stunned and sobbing, he cried out in disbelief, "The best race of my life! The best technique, the fastest. And I did it at 30!"

Five days later the old man amazed himself again. Going into Tokyo, Lewis had won 65 straight long jump competitions over a couple of generations of opponents. Now his archrival was Mike Powell, 27, the 1988 Olympic silver medalist. For 23 years, long jumpers had been consistently falling far short of Bob Beamon's world record of 29'2½". Only Lewis had been a real threat. But on this misty night in Tokyo, it was Powell, not Lewis, who beat Beamon: On his fifth try he soared 29'4½".

Lewis had two jumps left. Unbelievably, he very nearly delivered the impossible dream. While Powell watched anxiously, Lewis responded by leaping 29'1¼"—the best he had ever done. On his last try he soared 29' flat—the second best he had ever done.

At first Lewis spoke of Powell's feat with condescension: "Mike had the one great jump. He may never do it again." Later he praised Powell's form and said he deserved the record. So the question remained: Who is the real Carl Lewis?

OLYMPIC RESUME: *In 1984 Carl Lewis became the first man since Jesse Owens to win four track and field gold medals at a single Games. Four years later he won two more to bring his total to six.*

SOME CALLED HIM THE Baryshnikov of diving. His adoptive father said, "I see him as a bird." When young Louganis himself was asked what he most resembled, he thought for a moment, then said, "A panther."

He was adopted in 1960 at nine months. His natural father was Samoan, his mother European; both were 15 years old when he was born. His adoptive father, Peter Louganis, was in the fishing business, his adoptive mother, Frances, was a Texas farmer's daughter. They lived in El Cajon, California, not far from San Diego, and they named the dark-eyed baby Gregory Efthimios Louganis. Even as a tot he showed an acrobatic talent, so they put him in dance class, and at three he sang and tap-danced in a show, wearing a tiny tuxedo and top hat. He so loved the applause that he stayed on the stage, waiting for more, after the curtain came down. Despite such high points, his childhood was hardly idyllic. He stuttered terribly, was dyslexic and for a time was considered retarded. Children called him "nigger," and class bullies beat him up regularly.

He continued dance lessons but also became expert at tumbling and acrobatics. Not yet nine, he began to do tricks off the diving board in the Louganis's backyard pool. When he was 11, he competed at the Junior Olympics in Colorado Springs, where he caught the eye of Dr. Sammy Lee, the venerable platform diving champion of the 1948 and 1952 Olympics. "When I first watched him," recalled Lee, "I said to myself, 'My god, that's the greatest talent I've ever seen!'" In 1975 Greg's father asked Lee, a practicing physician who also ran the diving program at Mission Viejo, California, how much he would charge to coach Greg. "I don't charge anything," said Lee. "I do it for love. But listen, he'll have to live up to these requirements: No smoking, no drinking, and I want my home pool cleaned regularly."

In the early years Louganis fell short of Lee's expectations. "There was a lot of chicken in Greg then," Lee told GQ magazine. "He was young and sensitive, and he feared me. I had a tough attitude with most kids, but

with Greg I couldn't say things that might hurt him. I was more like a father to him. When he told me how he had been discriminated against because he was Samoan, I told him how I suffered discrimination because I was Korean. Tears came to his eyes. But you know, that boy has become the greatest diver ever in this sport. Why, when I went to China, they asked me if I knew the secret to Greg Louganis. I told them, 'Nobody knows the secret to Greg Louganis.'"

Louganis's own version of the secret went like this: "You just follow your instincts. When you're in the air, you have something like a cat's sense. You're aware of where your body is going, and your peripheral vision tells you how high off the water you are, so you can plan your dive and your entry. If you are diving well, you have all the time in the world to attend to the details."

Louganis won a silver medal in Montreal at the age of 16, but because of the U.S. boycott, he couldn't compete in Moscow. Still, by the time the Los Angeles Games rolled around, he had won 26 U.S., four Pan American and three world titles. In L.A. he became the first man in 56 years to win gold in both springboard and platform diving. Four years later he repeated the feat at the Seoul Games—despite a sore shoulder, a case of sinusitis and a five-stitch cut on his head from smacking it on the springboard during a preliminary round.

He retired within a year, saying, "I just want to be an employed actor." He read for parts in *Spaceballs* and *Prince Valium* and came up empty. A year after Seoul he played the dashing prince—replete with crown and epaulets—in a Long Beach Civic Light Opera production of *Cinderella*. He waltzed and sang, and afterward an old show-biz pro in the cast, Alan Young of *Mr. Ed* fame, gave Louganis high marks: "He's a natural Prince Charming. He's handsome and he looks great in a white suit."

OLYMPIC RESUME: *With victories in platform and springboard diving in 1984 and '88, Greg Louganis became the only man to sweep both diving events in back-to-back Olympics.*

AS A CHILD IN DAYTON, HE launched homemade rockets, dissected frogs and delivered newspapers. In high school he was a budding artist and played the sax in the all-city orchestra. His father was a science and math teacher and an elementary school principal. His mother was a supervisor of instruction for the public school system. He was small throughout his adolescence—5' 8", 135 pounds as a high school senior. He wore glasses and braces, and the kids called him Cagey or Metalmouth.

Schmid, a West German. That was the last time he tasted defeat for nine years, nine months and nine days— a span that encompassed 107 consecutive races. Included in the streak was another gold medal in Los Angeles and a world record of 47.02 seconds that was still standing in 1992. So exquisite was his form that Dr. Dick Hill of Southern University, another hurdling coach, said, "Compared to Ed, everyone else looked like roosters with their tails on fire."

He entered Morehouse College in Atlanta on an academic scholarship and went out for track, concentrating on the 110-meter high hurdles and the 400-meter run. He was mediocre. Then on March 26, 1976, just four months before the Montreal Olympics, everything changed. He was competing at the Florida Relays and he ran the 110 highs, the 400 flat and, for the first time, one of the most difficult events in track, the 400-meter intermediate hurdles. He ran it in 50.1 seconds—not good enough to win. However, Dr. Leroy Walker, the U.S. Olympic track coach that year and a former hurdler himself, saw Moses perform that day. "Anybody who knew anything about hurdling could see that if they were pointing this guy to something other than the 400 intermediates, they had the wrong race," he said later. "His size and his speed; his base, the ability to carry the stride; his 'skim,' what we call the measurement of the stride over the hurdle—he had it all."

Indeed. In Montreal, Edwin Moses won with ease and became an instant star. He always raced in opaque dark glasses, and many people thought he was a sinister presence. "I know it was difficult to relate to me back then," he said. "I was black, studying physics and engineering. I was from a small school nobody ever heard of. A guy who took up this race and four months later won the gold medal. All this was a fantasy. Then the sunglasses. And they wanted to make me more of a fantasy. But did anybody stop to ask if the sunglasses were prescription? My eyes have been sensitive to light since the fifth grade. Without glasses I can't see the next hurdle."

On Aug. 26, 1977, Moses lost a race in Berlin to Harald

As his winning streak grew, he became a household name. His autograph was a collector's item, consisting of *Edwin Moses...400...47.02* and a line drawing of a hurdle. He was a friend of Bill Cosby's. He was chairman of the USOC's committee on substance abuse. His California license plate read OLYMPYN. He was making at least $500,000 a year from endorsements and track promoters who paid him $20,000 per appearance.

Finally, on June 4, 1987, he was beaten, finishing a scant .13 of a second behind Danny Harris, the silver medalist from the L.A. Games. "I wasn't disappointed," he said. "It was just destiny. The streak was made concrete by the loss. I went right back to my training program." He was 33, but he won 10 more straight, and by the time the Seoul Olympics arrived, he was favored for another gold.

But this time he lost, finishing third for the bronze medal. He was remarkably easy in defeat. "I've lost before, and I've come back," he said. "The other guys just ran their best races, and I didn't. I know it was the Olympic Games, but for me it was just a normal business day. For them it was the chance of a lifetime."

As for Edwin Moses, he had become an American institution rather early in life. As Dr. Walker said: "He's gone past the textbooks now. In an art gallery, do we stand around talking about Van Gogh? Extraordinary talent is obvious. We're in the rarefied presence of an immortal here."

OLYMPIC RESUME: *Edwin Moses won the 400-meter hurdles in 1976 and '84, by which time he had won 102 straight races and run 27 of the 32 sub-48 second times recorded in his event.*

HE WAS ALWAYS A SWEDE through and through—stoic, silent, as remote as the arctic mountains he grew up in more than 1,000 miles north of Stockholm. He spent his first six years on his grandparents' farm outside the village of Tärnaby (pop. 600). This was a bitter land, where the sun shone for no more than half an hour during the shortest days of winter. It was a lonely place, too, and his only playmates were a few Lapp children who lived nearby. Young Ingemar turned to skiing because, "It was a thing I could do alone." When he reached school age he moved to the village to live with his parents, though he remained withdrawn and shy and still had few friends.

But he continued to ski, tutored by his father, who was a fan of ski racing, and he became a grim and hardheaded competitor, usually able to win, but racked by furious sobs when he couldn't. Hermann Nogler, the Italian trainer who was Stenmark's coach throughout his career, first laid eyes on him when Ingemar was 13—and his promise fairly glowed. "I watched him for a week," Nogler recalled, "and I said to myself, 'That boy will be a world champion.' You could see the natural talent, the single-mindedness, the way he was hard on himself." True enough. When Ingemar Stenmark emerged from those dark Swedish winters, he was a prodigy.

At 17 he joined the blue-ribbon World Cup ski racing circuit, and the following year he was in contention for the overall championship (slalom, giant slalom and downhill results combined) going into the final race of the season. In a dramatic head-to-head slalom, the upstart teenager might have won the title except that he slipped at the last gate and finished just behind the great Italian Gustavo Thoeni, who had already won three World Cup championships in his four years of competition. Then in 1976 Stenmark won the overall World Cup, won it again in '77 and '78, and in '79 he set a single-season record of 13 victories—one more than Jean-Claude Killy had amassed in 1967.

Stenmark was now very famous and quite rich, but it certainly didn't turn him into a playboy. Nogler said, "He does not smoke, drink, dance, womanize—in short, he has no private life." His new celebrity did bring about one change, though: His father and mother decided to get married because of it. In the harsh life of the Swedish arctic, niceties such as marriage before children were not closely observed. But with their son in the spotlight, it seemed only fitting for the couple to legalize their relationship and legitimize their son, and they did so in a civil ceremony.

By the time the 1980 Winter Olympics rolled around, the spotlight was glaring, for Stenmark was on another super-skiing spree, this one featuring 14 consecutive giant slalom wins. Some compared this accomplishment to Joe DiMaggio's 56-game hitting streak in 1941, and TIME magazine called him "the Alpine equivalent of DiMaggio [with] the same gift for doing the impossible in an unhurried, almost languid, offhandedly elegant manner." At Lake Placid he won both of his golds by solid margins—.50 of a second in the slalom and a spectacular .95 of a second in the giant slalom, marking his 15th straight victory in that event.

There has never been another Alpine skier like Stenmark. He competed in 270 World Cup events and won 86 of them—a winning percentage of more than 31%. Closest to him in total wins were the Austrian grande dame Annemarie Moser-Pröll with 62 and the multitalented Swiss Pirmin Zurbriggen with 40. Stenmark retired in 1989 at the age of 33 after 16 years of competition, knowing that his records were not likely to be broken—ever.

Given all the glory, he made an odd remark after he quit: "If I could start my life all over again, I wouldn't have become a slalom skier. I would have gone for a team sport. Then you don't have to be the best all the time to enjoy it. And the team can be good even if you have a bad day. You can share everything with others, success as well as failures. I think it's nicer to compete in a team sport."

OLYMPIC RESUME: *In 1980 Ingemar Stenmark won the slalom and giant slalom in Lake Placid. He is one of only four men to win both events at a single Olympic Games.*

HER DESCRIPTION OF HOW one performs a perfect aerial flip on a balance beam went like this: "You should go *blam!* — so solid that you shake the arena." As it turned out, this also happened to be the best way to describe the impression Mary Lou Retton herself made on the world during her heroics at the Los Angeles Olympics. *Blam!* and the arena shook.

She was 16 and tiny, of course — 4' 9", 95 pounds, size 1 dress, size 3 shoes. SPORTS ILLUSTRATED's Bob Ottum wrote before the

Games: "If there were such a thing as the Official Pixie of the 1984 Olympic Games, this girl would be it. The story is that she was born in a small West Virginia town, and you can believe it if you want to, but there's better reason to suspect that she simply stepped out from under a toadstool one day in 1968. Scale-model leotards and all."

Her effervescence was like a force of nature, and she burbled on and on in a stream of the bluntest, liveliest, funniest quotes any athlete ever uttered. In explaining the balletic tiptoe steps gymnasts use onstage, she said, "That stuff's just for show, to make us look classier than we really are. Ordinarily we all walk like little bitty football players." She explained the secret of her success this way: "It's all in the training. I work at this seven days a week — two long, hard sessions a day, drilling myself. Constantly. And at night sometimes I dream gymnastic dreams. I'll be lying there quietly, sound asleep, and suddenly my whole body will give a great big jump and practically throw me out of bed. Here's what it takes to be a complete gymnast: Someone should be able to sneak up and drag you out at midnight and push you out on some strange floor, and you should be able to do your entire routine sound asleep in your pajamas. *Without one mistake.*"

After she performed her perfect last-chance execution of a full-twisting layout Tsukahara vault in L.A., she cried out in glee, "I stuck it!" And after she stepped out of the Olympic Village for the first time following that victory, she gasped, "I mean, there were mobs of people. And the people knew me! They said things like, 'Mary Lou, you've been in our home. You've been in our living room. We feel like we *know* you, Mary Lou!' I mean, I'd understand people recognizing me if I had purple hair or something, but I'm just a normal teenager. I'm still just Mary Lou."

More like Mary Lou, Inc. After L.A. she was flooded with endorsement offers, and she signed contracts with 10 different corporations, each paying an estimated $100,000 to $200,000 a year, including McDonald's, Vidal Sassoon, Wheaties, Super Juice frozen juice bars and Energizer batteries. She produced her own exercise video, published an autobiography and appeared in a series of exercise spots called Funfit, which were interspersed through Saturday morning cartoons on ABC.

Her radiant smile turned up so often on packages and in commercials that some people thought she had overdone it. In 1986 Johnny Carson held up a box of Wheaties with her picture on the front and said to his audience, "Nothing against Miss Retton, personally, but when I get up in the morning I wake up with the grumps. I do not want to look at a box with somebody *perky* [on it]. What do you think, folks?" The audience roared, "Trash it!" and Carson crushed the cereal box in a trash compactor to loud cheers.

Retton retired from competition in 1986 but returned to serious training in 1989 to prepare for a U.S. tour with Olga Korbut. Soon she was thinking about competing for real in the 1992 Games, until — inevitably — the truth dawned: "I just can't do it. My body's strong enough, but I don't have the discipline. The girl who won those medals was a machine." Did she have regrets about the sacrifices she had made to win the gold? "You give up your childhood. You miss proms and games and high school events, and people say it's awful. I don't know. I mean, I walked on top of the Great Wall of China when I was in eighth grade. I rode the bullet train in Japan. I met Gorbachev. I met Michael Jackson. I say it was a good trade. You miss something, but I think I gained more than I lost."

OLYMPIC RESUME: *With her victory in the all-around, Mary Lou Retton became the first U.S. woman to win an individual Olympic medal in gymnastics.*

KRISTIN OTTO

ON NOVEMBER 10, 1989, THE day the Berlin Wall came tumbling down and East Germany became free, Kristin Otto wrote in the diary she had kept for more than nine years: "A day which will become history because it is the coronation of all that has gone before. As of today, the borders are open. All hell has broken loose at the visa offices and the banks. Everybody wants to seize this moment because all have been waiting for it for so very long, the moment when they are at last free to travel...." To make the date stand out from the less cosmic days, she highlighted it with brightly colored felt pens—just as she had marked another special entry, on Sept. 15, 1988, the day she won her historic sixth gold medal in swimming at the Seoul Olympics.

Calling her feat historic is no exaggeration, for Otto's six broke the record for most Olympic golds won by any woman in any sport—ever. But for a cruel twist of world politics, Otto might have won more gold medals than *any* Olympian of the modern era—more than Paavo Nurmi's nine, more even than Ray Ewry's 10 with the rump Games of '06 included.

In 1982 Otto was 16, and she won three world championship golds. In 1983 she became the first female to break one minute in the 100-meter backstroke at 59.97. In 1984, she rose to the top of her sport, set world records in the 100- and 200-meter freestyles and was named woman swimmer of the year. Had the world been sane she would have gone to the Los Angeles Games favored to win five gold medals on the strength of her past performances. But the Soviet Union with all of its satellites, including the G.D.R., was boycotting the L.A. Olympics in retaliation for the U.S. boycott of Moscow in 1980. Neither of these feckless acts made any real difference to either of the superpower combatants. But they did profound damage to would-be Olympic heroes and heroines such as Otto. To add injury to insult, later that year she also cracked a vertebra and developed excruciating back pain from a pinched nerve. For nine months she wore a neck brace and didn't enter the water at all. At last her doctors told her that she must plan to live her life without sports.

Had she believed them she might well have vanished into obscurity. Instead, when the pain subsided she went swimming and was aghast to find that the backstroke triggered a sharp, debilitating shock of pain in her cervical vertebrae. Frightened, she turned over, tried the freestyle stroke and, miraculously, found she could do it without pain. She set out to get back in shape for the 1986 world championships in Madrid. She won six medals there, four of them gold, and the versatility of her performance was something to behold: She medaled in every kind of competitive stroke there was.

In Seoul she won gold medals in three different swimming styles—freestyle, backstroke and butterfly. No Olympian ever—not Johnny Weissmuller, not Mark Spitz, not Kornelia Ender—had done such a thing. She surprised even herself: "I didn't come here with a plan to win many gold medals, just one or two. I'm happy and quite frankly astonished."

She went back behind the Wall after the Seoul Games and retired from swimming. When freedom burst upon East Germany late in '89, she emerged as a butterfly from a cocoon. Always physically beautiful and amazingly graceful despite her 6'¾" height, she now boasted a dazzling smile and a radiant personality. She was studying to be a broadcast journalist, and she seemed born to be a star there, too.

Later, when East German coaches confessed in 1991 to having fed steroids to all of their swimmers, she responded fiercely: "I get very angry when athletes bear the burden. No one can take my success in Seoul away from me. I was like Mark Spitz, lucky to have a great gift, and those six medals were the result of many years' work. It is important to research what really happened, to ask officials what they did. I passed drug tests, but I can't be sure what was put into my drinks and food."

OLYMPIC RESUME: *In 1988 swimmer Kristin Otto won six gold medals, the most ever won by any woman at a single Games.*

HE WAS NAMED FRANCIS Morgan Thompson, born to a Nigerian father and Scottish mother in the Notting Hill Gate section of London. Oddly enough the house was already full of males named Frank—his father Frank, his brother Franklin and his other brother, also Francis ("I guess they just couldn't think of any other name," said Thompson). So Frank Sr., a member of the Ibo tribe, gave his youngest an African nickname, Ayodele. It got shortened to Dele and eventually changed some more to Daley.

Ayodele translates literally to "joy enters the house," but this wasn't quite the case with the baby Daley Thompson. "That child was a terror from the minute he was born," his mother recalled. When he was seven he was such a handful that he was sent to Farney Close, a boarding school for troubled children about 40 miles south of London. "Of course, I didn't want to leave home," Thompson said. "But it ended up just great. That's the story of my life. I always seem to fall into shit and come up smellin' o' roses." He turned to sports—first soccer, then track—and it was all roses. A Farney Close teacher recalled, "He had that automatic feel for running. And when he learned to jump, it was the same thing. Physically he was very gifted. But mentally he had that bit of vital grind, or whatever it is, a mental toughness. He was never vicious, but he never let up. Going, always going."

Thompson entered his first decathlon in Cwmbran, Wales, in 1975 when he was 16 and won with 6,685 points—an astonishing 2,000 more than the British record for his age group. At 17 he qualified for the Olympics in Montreal—the youngest decathlete since Bob Mathias in 1948. Thompson finished 18th but used his time at the Games to study Bruce Jenner's world-record performance. "If I were the kind of person to be impressed," Thompson said, "Jenner would have impressed me. He looked relaxed and under control, rattling off one personal best after another. But I saw that, well, he wasn't that talented physically. He was just a hard worker. I learned that from him, the necessity of it."

In Moscow Thompson won by a relatively tight 164 points over the Soviet Yuri Kutsenko, and in Los Angeles he defeated the West German Jürgen Hingsen by 125 points—matching Mathias's feat of winning two straight Olympic decathlons. Thompson's post–gold medal antics were almost as memorable as his results. In Moscow he was asked what his plans for the future were and he said, "What will I do now? Why, films, blue movies." In Los Angeles he ran a victory lap wearing a T-shirt that said on the front THANKS AMERICA FOR A GOOD GAMES AND A GREAT TIME, and on the back, BUT WHAT ABOUT THE TV COVERAGE?—which referred to ABC's ham-handed America-first emphasis. Again Daley was asked about his plans, and he replied, "Oh, I don't know. Settling down, kids...." Then someone said, "Daley, two questions: What did Princess Anne say to you after you'd won? And who's going to be the mother of your kids?" Quickly he answered, "Well, you've just mentioned the lady. And the answer to the first question is, she said, 'I hope they'll be white.'" On the victory stand he jauntily whistled along with the band playing *God Save the Queen*.

Four years later he went to the Games in Seoul, but he injured himself in a pole-vaulting fall and finished fourth. That was his last decathlon, although in 1991 he talked of trying to qualify for his fourth Olympics in Barcelona.

Thompson always insisted that the decathlon was its own satisfaction: "You're always being asked about the supposed irrationality of the decathlon. People who don't do it can't see the reward equaling the price.... To train hard is enough satisfaction in its own right. Whatever kind of athlete you are, say, a distance runner even, when you're running eight hard half miles in your best average time for that workout, you know it's great. You can't feel that every day, but I do 10 events. There's always somewhere to get excited. I love the decathlon for the way it brings out your character."

OLYMPIC RESUME: *With victories in 1980 and '84, Daley Thompson became the only man other than Bob Mathias to win gold medals in the decathlon in back-to-back Olympics.*

THE ARGUMENT IN CALGARY over her provocative costumes got a little bitchy. The coach of a rival skater accused Katarina Witt of "exploiting herself" and carped that her outfit belonged in "a circus. All that's missing is the horse and reins. We're here to skate in a dress, not in a G-string." At which point Fräulein Witt fired off a very widely quoted retort, "I think every man prefers looking at a well-built woman [rather] than someone built in the shape of a ball. Why not stress what we have that is attractive?"

So she proceeded to skate in a stressful little thing that was cut exceedingly high at the hips, and she wore so much lady-is-a-tramp makeup that some thought she had gone too far. As it turned out, she had. In a 1991 interview with *Vogue,* she said, "I was so nervous. I was putting my makeup on in the Olympic Village, and then I went to the ice rink and did my warming up. Because I was so nervous, I kept going back into the bathroom for more makeup. When I saw the picture, I thought, Oh, my god, Katarina!" The revealing costumes, however, were definitely not a mistake. "I have the boobs and I have the butt. I'm lucky the proportions are right. Your butt builds up through skating," she said. "I'm an athlete not a model. What could I do if I'm too skinny?"

Her gold medals in Sarajevo and Calgary made her the most glamorous sports star in the notably unglamorous environs of East Germany. She was coddled and cared for like a queen bee—and they did indeed call her Katarina the Great. She was given the usual socialist perks: luxury apartment in the city, vacation dacha in the country, car, money, travel. "I was privileged," she told *Vogue.* "I really thought I deserved it. I am a little bit spoiled."

After the Berlin Wall fell in late '89, Witt was ambivalent about the reunification of the two Germanies. She said, "Everyone is talking Germany! Germany! They are not my feelings. My country is not the Germany of 60 or 70 years ago. It is *East* Germany." She even equated the mighty East German sports machine with Western free enterprise: "The sports system in East Germany worked like the economy does here. The best person goes forward." And she was particularly troubled by the thought of rich Germans from the West swarming in to take over her homeland. "They will buy up every centimeter. The country I know won't be here anymore. It won't exist. And this hurts." Soon she had her first distasteful contacts with pushy opportunists. First her country place was burglarized of an estimated $60,000 in jewelry, and then a typically brassy Western tabloid hired a crane to lift a photographer up eight stories so he could shoot directly into her Berlin apartment. "Can you imagine this?" she said.

However fondly she recalled her socialist past, capitalism certainly seemed to agree with her. Once retired, she began performing on a lucrative tour of Western Europe and the U.S. with Brian Boitano, the 1988 men's gold medalist. She also starred with Boitano in a generally praised HBO film called *Carmen on Ice.* In the spring of '91 she signed with Du Pont to be what *The New Yorker* called a "spokesmodel" for a line of sports products. At a Rockefeller Center press conference, she both modeled (an outfit made of Lycra and Micromattique) and spoke ("Since Lycra provides complete freedom of movement, it's one fiber I rely on when I perform"). She had lunch with Donald Trump, the fallen New York tycoon, who was said to have fallen hard for her. And she landed a multi-year contract with the CBS network to be a "spokeskater" who would both commentate and demonstrate her expertise in her sport. She did well in this role during the Albertville Games.

As she proved in her soaring, high-pressure Olympic gold medal performances, she was born to be a star—whether the firmament is socialist or capitalist. She said it best herself: "It doesn't matter where I am. If I feel eyes on me, I'm better."

OLYMPIC RESUME: *With gold medals in 1984 and '88, Katarina Witt became the first woman since Sonja Henie in 1932 to win two straight Olympic titles in women's figure skating.*

SHE HARDLY SEEMED DES-tined for Olympic stardom—especially stardom in the newest, glitziest, noisiest event to be added to the Games in the 20th century. Shy, stocky and raised in a New Jersey suburb, she once waited tables at a pasta joint in Vermont, yearned to play the saxophone and adored doing fashion sketches. In describing her college days at the Ridge-wood School of Art and Design in New Jersey, she admitted, "I never went to the sharp pencil and a ruler. I headed more toward the abstract. That's me."

She definitely headed more toward the abstract when it came to describing her Olympic specialty—a previously little-known and less-understood event called mogul ski-ing. At one time or another, Weinbrecht called mogul ski-ing "a rush," a search for "a dream run" and "the motocross of winter." In fact, it involves descending a steep hill at high speed over snow-covered bumps that range in size from "buried coffee tables to buried Volks-wagens," as Weinbrecht puts it. On the way down, com-petitors are required to perform a couple of airborne tricks with names like daffies, kosaks, zudniks, heli-copters, spread eagles, etc. The entire event is accompa-nied by deafening rock music, and at the end of each run, judges render subjective verdicts on the quality of the run and the performance of the tricks.

To the skeptics it seemed more like an updated version of '60s performance art than an Olympic sport. But then came the gloomy morning of Feb. 13, 1992, in Tignes, France, with a howling crowd of 10,000 assembled in a blinding snowstorm and many millions more tuned in on TV in more comfortable climes. And it was here that Donna Weinbrecht showed the multitudes precisely what mogul skiing was all about—and there was nothing abstract about it. It was pure hard muscle, brute courage and true grit.

In fact, her run was a landmark performance, even heroic in its way. This was the first time that mogul skiing—one of the three disciplines within freestyle skiing— was an offi-cial Olympic sport, and she was under crushing pressure to win. She had won two sea-son titles in World Cup mogul competition and had been ballyhooed for weeks before the Albertville Games as one of the few Americans with a remote chance of win-ning a medal.

But none of that affected this unflappable 26 year old. She entered the start gate and peered through the storm down the 253-meter field of daunting bumps. She recalled later, "The pressure was there. I couldn't fool myself. I was expected to win. My thoughts were on the kids who wrote me letters. To be brave. To be right here and now, not somewhere else. To ski right there. To be in the gate."

Maybe all that simple, kid-style advice did the trick. She flitted down the bone-rattling run in what looked to the unpracticed eye like a definite dream run—perhaps even a dream *rush*. Her magnificent descent to victory was accompanied by the pounding beat of Robert Gordon's *Rock Billy Boogie* and by a growing roar of wonder from the masses as she careened down the course that had been nicknamed Moon Base Zero by American skiers. Wein-brecht's triumph was a classic in all regards, and it proved that her sport belonged in the Olympics.

Such acceptance had been a long time in coming, partic-ularly from the hidebound Olympic traditionalists who believed that freestyle skiing had always been based on the moon and should stay there. Indeed, when the sport first appeared in the early '70s, it definitely had a hallu-cinogenic full-moon quality to it. Rules were spacey, tricks were outasight, competitors were flattered to be called hot dogs, and it was all a matter of "just hootin' and hollerin' and gettin' high," as one veteran recalled.

All that was ancient history after the Albertville Olympics. However, when Donna Weinbrecht described how she felt after her gold medal run, there was perhaps an inadvertent echo of highs past. "Very serene," she said. "In bliss."

OLYMPIC RESUME: *In 1992 Donna Weinbrecht won the first gold medal in the newly recognized sport of mogul skiing.*

ALBERTO TOMBA

IN 1988 A VETERAN TOMBA watcher from Bologna, journalist Leo Turrini, described the young man this way: "Alberto is like E.T. He doesn't realize the world is complicated. He thinks everyone is clean and honest, like he is. He has a big conscience. In all these years he has never said a bad thing about his teammates."

High praise. However, it could also be added that he has never said a bad thing about himself. He once joked to journalists: "I feel a little bit lonely out in front all the time. Maybe the other guys should start training a little more to try and catch up." Another time he vigorously beat his chest as he crossed the finish first and later explained, "I was so happy, I had to congratulate myself." After a string of victories he blurted to a journalist at Madonna di Campiglio, "I am the new messiah of skiing."

Some austere types on the World Cup circuit found Tomba's effusiveness offensive, but in general he was widely liked—precisely what he had in mind. Indeed, he once expressed the belief that, to some extent, his success depended on his being funny: "I'm considered the clown of my team because I cannot be serious for two minutes. I'm afraid if I become more serious I will stop winning. This is my character and I cannot change."

He was born to la dolce vita. His family home was a 16th-century villa with a tennis court, a kennel and a manicured labyrinth of gardens with a circular fountain and a marble cupid spouting water. It was located alone atop a hill above the village of Castel de' Britti. Tomba's father, Franco, owned an exclusive men's clothing store in Bologna that had passed through three generations of Tombas. After Alberto's Calgary triumphs, Franco bought him a Ferrari.

At times Tomba seemed to be living out the worst possible lazy playboy scenario: He grew fat, soft, careless in his skiing. His record in World Cup races was wildly uneven: In the Calgary Olympic season he won nine of the 18 races, but the following year he won only one, and in 1990–91 he fell in five slaloms, won no World Cup titles and no medals at the world championships. Then he sim-ply exploded into the '91–92 season, winning seven of his 14 races before Albertville.

Even in his slowest, fattest days, no one doubted his talent. The greatest slalom specialist of them all, Ingemar Stenmark, looked around him when he retired in 1989 and said, "Today there is only Tomba." Tomba's coach was Gustavo Thoeni, the former Italian hero who won four overall World Cups and a gold medal in the GS in Sapporo in '72 but was as colorless as dust compared to Tomba. Thoeni said, "He succeeds in transmitting to the skis his dynamite…. Even if he is undisciplined—and often I close both my eyes—I must admit that ultimately he has matured."

In the summer before Albertville, Tomba undertook a killing physical regime that reduced his body fat to a very lean 11.2 percent. He embarked on a rigorous program running slalom gates, and he came to be as hard as a steel spike. "Before I just used to throw myself into it, I would win and joke about it. I was a boy who thought life was a joke. Now I've grown up," he said.

It was just as well, for it was widely assumed in Albertville that Tomba would become the first Alpine skier to repeat double golds in consecutive Games. In a diary he wrote for *La Gazzetta dello Sport*, he confessed that before the giant slalom in Val d'Isère: "I was pretending to be confident, saying that these were the Alberto-ville Olympics. But inside I wasn't at all sure, believe me." That was hard to believe as he attacked the course with his deceptively elegant style and seemed to ride effortlessly to victory on a wave of noise from thousands of Tomba-mad Italians.

His second attempt for gold in the slalom missed—but barely. He wound up with the silver after a forlorn (for him) first run, followed by a brilliant, surging second run that left him a bare .28 of a second behind the winner. He flopped down on his back in the finish area, waggling his skis in the air and grinning impishly—not unlike E.T.

OLYMPIC RESUME: *In the 1988 and '92 Games, Alberto Tomba won two gold medals in the giant slalom and a silver and a gold in the slalom.*

ONCE UPON A TIME, IN 1936, A CENTURY AGO, A GREAT

CONTROVERSY RAGED OVER WHETHER BERLIN

SHOULD BE ALLOWED TO HOST THE OLYMPIC GAMES BECAUSE OF

HITLER'S NOTORIOUS POLICIES OF ANTI-SEMITISM. AT THE TIME THE

PRESIDENT OF THE IOC WAS A BELGIAN NAMED HENRI DE BAILLET-LATOUR, WHO

COUNTERED THE ANTI-BERLIN OUTCRY WITH A VERY STRANGE NOTION. "THE

OLYMPIC GAMES ARE NOT HELD IN BERLIN, IN LOS ANGELES OR IN AMSTERDAM," he said. "When the five-circled Olympic flag is raised over the stadium it becomes sacred Olympic territory, and theoretically and for all practical purposes the Games are held in ancient Olympia. There, I am the master."

It sounded like pompous hogwash in 1936, but now it turns out that Baillet-Latour had it right all the time. The Olympic movement, vintage 2036, does indeed operate out of "sacred territory," which is the official definition (for tax purposes) of the massive theme park in Greece known as OlympiaLand. But there is no single "master" of this environment, as Baillet-Latour envisioned. OlympiaLand is owned and operated by a unique consortium of eight organizations, each of which is the world's most expert and innovative institution in some specialized Olympic-oriented pursuit. Their expertise ranges from sports marketing to world peacekeeping, from soft-drink merchandising to theme park and sacred territory management, from TV production to worldwide packaging of the ancient conflict: good versus evil. The institutions in charge of these specialties, respectively, are: the International Management Group, the National Football League, the United Nations, Coca-Cola, the Walt Disney Company, the International Olympic Committee, Home Box Office and the Vatican.

OlympiaLand as we know it today in 2036 covers most of southern Greece, a 10,000-square-mile sprawl of new and ancient architecture approximately the size of the state of Maryland. About 250,000 eager Olympia Lads and Olympia Lasses live in Olympia-Land year-round to serve and entertain the 25 million visitors who pump $12.5 billion a year into the overflowing coffers of the Olympic movement. As the Olympic edicts of old decreed, amateurism is the rule among OlympiaLand employees, who take an oath vowing to work only for the love of their jobs. They are very good at what they do, but even the most fervent OlympiaLand fans comment on the slightly off-putting cultist quality of Olympia Lads and Lasses, many of whom have the Orphan Annie–eyed look once common among the Moonies and Hari Krishnas of the late 20th century.

The sacred territory is split into seven divisions, each with its own distinctive form of entertainment. There is *Old Ancient OlympiaLand*, where the crumbling stadiums, monuments and statuary of the original Greek competitions still stand as a living museum. Next door is *New Ancient OlympiaLand*, a vast space filled with tasteful replicas of the original venues equipped with thousands of seats, so modern spectators can witness in person recreated events from the olden Games, such as chariot races, footraces among armed men and the pancration. True to ancient practice, all competitions are performed by male athletes in the nude. When OlympiaLand first opened, only male spectators were allowed to attend, as was also dictated by ancient Olympic tradition. But the stadiums were nearly empty and losing money, so management said to hell with tradition and ordered the competitions opened to female spectators. The first month alone, 10,000 busloads of women descended on *New Ancient OlympiaLand* and there were riots. A rigid system of ticket distribution was installed, and these exhibitions are now sold out for the next two years.

Opening CeremonyLand is another favorite among women—although children and many men like it too. There are seven large beautiful stadiums, each an architectural prize and each seating about 100,000 people. Every day of the week a different stadium is the site of a full-dress, full-scale Olympic opening ceremony. These are not cheap imitations. They feature parades of national athletes, bands, choirs, symphony orchestras, acres of folk dancers, jugglers, hoop dancers, a solemn torch-lighting, Olympic oath-taking, and on and on. Tickets for *Opening CeremonyLand* are also sold out for two years.

Another popular attraction is *Risen-AgainLand* a complex entirely filled with replicas of Olympic stadiums from each of the modern Games since they began in 1896. Here you can enter the stadium of your choice and call up your favorite Olympic immortals through virtual-reality software and watch—up close and personal—as your chosen immortals rise again to compete as they did long, long ago. You can follow along behind Jim Thorpe as he performs the decathlon in the Olympic stadium in Stockholm in 1912. You can trot behind Paavo Nurmi as he competes in one of his nine gold medal distance races in one of the Olympic stadiums he inhabited between 1920 and 1928. You can be at Ben Johnson's shoulder on the track of the Olympic stadium in Seoul when he wins the gold for the 100-meter dash as well as later when he loses it with a failed urine test for banned substances. *Risen-AgainLand* is a gigantic money-maker because of its popularity with the over-65 set—a group that now outnumbers all other segments of the world population by 5 to 1.

Dream Competition City is big with senior citizens, too, but it is even bigger with gamblers. Here one can settle all those arguments as to whether Lasse Viren would have won over Emil Zátopek, Johnny Weissmuller over Mark Spitz, Bob Mathias over Daley Thompson, etc. Through a sophisticated computer handicapping system, which equalizes dream rivals from different eras in terms of nutrition, conditioning, training techniques and the like, you can arrange any match race you desire and then watch it unfold before your eyes. As the computer sets up, let us say, the conditions for a long jump competition between Alvin Kraenzlein and Bob Beamon, it is also computing the precise odds on the outcome. Of course, there are Dream Competition betting windows everywhere, and the Olympic movement skims off millions every month.

OlympiaLand's *Kingdom of Games* is the TV production center for the myriad Olympic television game shows which are transmitted globally on a 24-hour basis. Visitors flock to fill the studios. The most popular shows are *Olympic Wheel of Fortune, Olympic Trivial Pursuit, Olympic Jeopardy, the Olympic Gong Show* (starring past and present members of the IOC) and *You Be the Olympian* in which couch potatoes compete against each other in a variety of Olympic events. Two billion people a day worldwide tune in to these syndicated game shows via OlympiaLand's pay-per-view TV network. At the infinitesimal average cost of one cent per viewer per show, this enterprise is by far the biggest money-maker in the entire Olympic movement.

But profit and fun aside, let's turn to the moral core and spiritual centerpiece of OlympiaLand—the busy complex known as *War Games World*. Here we have achieved the ultimate in mankind's quest for peace: We no longer cancel the Olympic Games when wars break out; we have canceled wars and replaced them with the Olympic Games!

It is true. Disputes between nations are now settled through sport, not combat. Here is how it works: *War Games World* contains every imaginable Olympic competitive environment—track and field stadiums, ice rinks, swimming and diving halls, equestrian fields, basketball arenas, boxing arenas, gymnastic arenas,

weightlifting halls, archery ranges, velodromes—the works. Every three months OlympiaLand's management schedules a full program of competition in all 70 official Olympic sports between teams from two "warring" nations. These countries may be locked in disagreement over a wide variety of issues—border disputes, trade inequities, ancient tribal differences, ethnic conflicts, matters relating to politics, economics, ideology, religion—whatever. No matter what the point of contention, the two countries' teams compete in a complex schedule involving every Olympic event. At the end the winner gets what it wants—or the two nations jointly decide to settle before the contest reaches its conclusion. Frequently a victory in a critical event will soften a once intractable negotiating stance.

There are, of course, rules intended to maximize fairness and equality in the competition. For example, OlympiaLand management insists that no more than 25% of a nation's team members can be paid, foreign-born ringers; the rest must be certifiable native citizens. Nevertheless, the inclusion of superstar athlete-mercenaries automatically upgrades the quality of competition and thus guarantees greater spectator appeal. And, as it has worked out, world superstars of one kind or another have competed in every War Game, even those involving the smallest, least developed countries. When Costa Rica challenged Honduras to an Olympic War Game over coastal fishing rights some time ago, the famed veteran athlete-mercenaries Michael Jordan and Larry Bird were hired to play basketball for Costa Rica and Honduras, respectively. In that same War Game, Boris Becker defeated Pete Sampras in a tennis match that ultimately won the day—and the fishing rights—for Honduras. (Unfortunately, all this traffic in jock-mercenaries means that athletes' agents have replaced arms dealers as our basic global power brokers. This is not an improvement.)

Once a conflict is joined in *War Games World*, sports competition goes on daily. Citizens of the warring countries flock to OlympiaLand to cheer on their warriors. Spectators from neutral nations also find the competition thrilling since the current world order can be completely upset by the result of a single Greco-Roman wrestling match. There are parimutuel betting windows everywhere at *War Games World*, and gamblers can wager on anything—point spreads in

games, time spreads in races, attendance at the water polo consolation match, etc. Of course, the Olympia-Land pay-per-view network beams all of the competitions worldwide.

Olympic War Games have produced important results. The long, nasty U.S.-Japan trade dispute was settled through War Games in 2008 when the daughter of Mary Lou Retton received a perfect 10 for a triple back Tsukahara vault, a score that forced Japan to drop its protectionist barrier against rice imports. The once bloody ethnic combat between Armenia and Azerbaijan was resolved in a dramatic series of fencing matches. And Iraq's Saddam Hussein was overthrown after an unknown ambidextrous Kurd Ping-Pong player defeated an Iraqi world champion with an attack that was all blazing forehands.

Olympic War Games go on throughout the year in OlympiaLand. However, every four years there is still a single big Olympic Games of the old-fashioned kind, with teams from most of the 1,210 nations that now exist in our atomized post–cold war world geography—a geography, by the way, that includes 50 separate nations from what was formerly the United States of America. The quadrennial Olympic Games are still moved from country to country around the globe. As you will recall, after 1992 the Winter and Summer Games were split so as to create an Olympic competition every other year. Soon, greed got the better of the Olympic pooh-bahs, and in the year 2000 they decreed there would be not only Summer and Winter Games, but also Spring and Fall Games—in other words, an Olympics every year.

This was a mistake. Boredom reigned, TV ratings plummeted, sponsors quit. Alarmed, Olympic policy-makers acted fast to cut their losses. In 2016 they returned to the traditional four-year movable feast, which now occurs in only one season of the year—summer. Do we miss the Winter Games? Yes, but we have no choice: The greenhouse effect has melted away the last vestiges of winter in the world. As for the Spring Olympics, with its emphasis on gardening events and kite flying, and the Fall Olympics, which was dominated by leaf-raking and leaf-burning competitions—well, no one has missed them at all.

OLYMPIC GAMES SUMMARY

S U M M E R

	YEAR	SITE	DATES	COMPETITORS			MOST MEDALS	US MEDALS
				MEN	WOMEN	NATIONS		
I	1896	Athens	Apr 6-15	311	0	13	Greece (10-19-18—47)	11-6-2—19 (2nd)
II	1900	Paris	May 20-Oct 28	1319	11	22	France (29-41-32—102)	20-14-19—53 (2nd)
III	1904	St Louis	July 1-Nov 23	681	6	12	United States (80-86-72—238)	
—	1906	Athens	Apr 22-May 2	877	7	20	France (15-9-16—40)	12-6-5—23 (4th)
IV	1908	London	Apr 27-Oct 31	1999	36	23	Britain (56-50-39—145)	23-12-12—47 (2nd)
V	1912	Stockholm	May 5-July 22	2490	57	28	Sweden (24-24-17—65)	23-19-19—61 (2nd)
VI	1916	Berlin		Canceled because of war				
VII	1920	Antwerp	Apr 20-Sep 12	2543	64	29	United States (41-27-28—96)	
VIII	1924	Paris	May 4-July 27	2956	136	44	United States (45-27-27—99)	
IX	1928	Amsterdam	May 17-Aug 12	2724	290	46	United States (22-18-16—56)	
X	1932	Los Angeles	July 30-Aug 14	1281	127	37	United States (41-32-31—104)	
XI	1936	Berlin	Aug 1-16	3738	328	49	Germany (33-26-30—89)	24-20-12—56 (2nd)
XII	1940	Tokyo		Canceled because of war				
XIII	1944	London		Canceled because of war				
XIV	1948	London	July 29-Aug 14	3714	385	59	United States (38-27-19—84)	
XV	1952	Helsinki	July 19-Aug 3	4407	518	69	United States (40-19-17—76)	
XVI	1956	Melbourne*	Nov 22-Dec 8	2958	384	67	USSR (37-29-32—98)	32-25-17—74 (2nd)
XVII	1960	Rome	Aug 25-Sep 11	4738	610	83	USSR (43-29-31—103)	34-21-16—71 (2nd)
XVIII	1964	Tokyo	Oct 10-24	4457	683	93	United States (36-26-28—90)	
XIX	1968	Mexico City	Oct 12-27	4750	781	112	United States (45-28-34—107)	
XX	1972	Munich	Aug 26-Sep 10	5848	1299	122	USSR (50-27-22—99)	33-31-30—94 (2nd)
XXI	1976	Montreal	July 17-Aug 1	4834	1251	92✻	USSR (49-41-35—125)	34-35-25—94 (3rd)
XXII	1980	Moscow	July 19-Aug 3	4265	1088	81✶	USSR (80-69-46—195)	Did not compete
XXIII	1984	Los Angeles	July 28-Aug 12	5458	1620	141#	United States (83-61-30—174)	
XXIV	1988	Seoul	Sep 17-Oct 2	7105	2476	160	USSR (55-31-46—132)	36-31-27—94 (3rd)
XXV	1992	Barcelona	July 25-Aug 9	7555	3008	172	Unified Team (45-38-29—112)	37-34-37—108 (2nd)

*The equestrian events were held in Stockholm, Sweden, June 10-17, 1956.
✻This figure includes Cameroon, Egypt, Morocco, and Tunisia, countries that boycotted the 1976 Olympics after some of their athletes had already competed.
✶The US was among 65 countries that refused to participate in the 1980 Summer Games in Moscow.
#The USSR, East Germany, and 14 other countries skipped the Summer Games in Los Angeles.

W I N T E R

	YEAR	SITE	DATES	COMPETITORS			MOST MEDALS	US MEDALS
				MEN	WOMEN	NATIONS		
I	1924	Chamonix	Jan 25-Feb 4	281	13	16	Norway (4-7-6—17)	1-2-1—4 (3rd)
II	1928	St Moritz	Feb 11-19	468	27	25	Norway (6-4-5—15)	2-2-2—6 (2nd)
III	1932	Lake Placid	Feb 4-15	274	32	17	United States (6-4-2—12)	
IV	1936	Garmisch-Partenkirchen	Feb 6-16	675	80	28	Norway (7-5-3—15)	1-0-3—4 (T-5th)
—	1940	Garmisch-Partenkirchen		Canceled because of war				
—	1944	Cortina d'Ampezzo		Canceled because of war				
V	1948	St Moritz	Jan 30-Feb 8	636	77	28	Norway (4-3-3—10) Sweden (4-3-3—10) Switzerland (3-4-3—10)	3-4-2—9 (4th)
VI	1952	Oslo	Feb 14-25	623	109	30	Norway (7-3-6—16)	4-6-1—11 (2nd)
VII	1956	Cortina d'Ampezzo	Jan 26-Feb 5	686	132	32	USSR (7-3-6—16)	2-3-2—7 (T-4th)
VIII	1960	Squaw Valley	Feb 18-28	521	144	30	USSR (7-5-9—21)	3-4-3—10 (2nd)
IX	1964	Innsbruck	Jan 29-Feb 9	986	200	36	USSR (11-8-6—25)	1-2-3—6 (7th)
X	1968	Grenoble	Feb 6-18	1081	212	37	Norway (6-6-2—14)	1-5-1—7 (T-7th)
XI	1972	Sapporo	Feb 3-13	1015	217	35	USSR (8-5-3—16)	3-2-3—8 (6th)
XII	1976	Innsbruck	Feb 4-15	900	228	37	USSR (13-6-8—27)	3-3-4—10 (T-3rd)
XIII	1980	Lake Placid	Feb 14-23	833	234	37	USSR (10-6-6—22)	6-4-2—12 (3rd)
XIV	1984	Sarajevo	Feb 7-19	1002	276	49	USSR (6-10-9—25)	4-4-0—8 (T-5th)
XV	1988	Calgary	Feb 13-28	1128	317	57	USSR (11-9-9—29)	2-1-3—6 (T-8th)
XVI	1992	Albertville	Feb 8-23	1475	585	63	Germany (10-10-6—26)	5-4-2—11 (6th)

OLYMPIC CHAMPIONS

Note: OR=Olympic Record; WR=World Record; EOR=Equals Olympic Record; EWR=Equals World Record; WB=World Best.

SUMMER GAMES
TRACK AND FIELD
MEN

100 METERS

Year	Champion	Time
1896	Thomas Burke, United States	12.0
1900	Frank Jarvis, United States	11.0
1904	Archie Hahn, United States	11.0
1906	Archie Hahn, United States	11.2
1908	Reginald Walker, South Africa	10.8 OR
1912	Ralph Craig, United States	10.8
1920	Charles Paddock, United States	10.8
1924	Harold Abrahams, Great Britain	10.6 OR
1928	Percy Williams, Canada	10.8
1932	Eddie Tolan, United States	10.3 OR
1936	Jesse Owens, United States	10.3
1948	Harrison Dillard, United States	10.3
1952	Lindy Remigino, United States	10.4
1956	Bobby Morrow, United States	10.5
1960	Armin Hary, West Germany	10.2 OR
1964	Bob Hayes, United States	10.0 EWR
1968	Jim Hines, United States	9.95 WR
1972	Valery Borzov, USSR	10.14
1976	Hasely Crawford, Trinidad	10.06
1980	Allan Wells, Great Britain	10.25
1984	Carl Lewis, United States	9.99
1988	Carl Lewis, United States*	9.92 WR
1992	Linford Christie, Great Britain	9.96

*Ben Johnson, Canada, disqualified.

200 METERS

Year	Champion	Time
1900	John Walter Tewksbury, United States	22.2
1904	Archie Hahn, United States	21.6 OR
1906	Not held	
1908	Robert Kerr, Canada	22.6
1912	Ralph Craig, United States	21.7
1920	Allen Woodring, United States	22.0
1924	Jackson Scholz, United States	21.6
1928	Percy Williams, Canada	21.8
1932	Eddie Tolan, United States	21.2 OR
1936	Jesse Owens, United States	20.7 OR
1948	Mel Patton, United States	21.1
1952	Andrew Stanfield, United States	20.7
1956	Bobby Morrow, United States	20.6 OR
1960	Livio Berruti, Italy	20.5 EWR
1964	Henry Carr, United States	20.3 OR
1968	Tommie Smith, United States	19.83 WR
1972	Valery Borzov, USSR	20.00
1976	Donald Quarrie, Jamaica	20.23
1980	Pietro Mennea, Italy	20.19
1984	Carl Lewis, United States	19.80 OR
1988	Joe DeLoach, United States	19.75 OR
1992	Mike Marsh, United States	20.01

400 METERS

Year	Champion	Time
1896	Thomas Burke, United States	54.2
1900	Maxey Long, United States	49.4 OR
1904	Harry Hillman, United States	49.2 OR
1906	Paul Pilgrim, United States	53.2
1908	Wyndham Halswelle, Great Britain	50.0
1912	Charles Reidpath, United States	48.2 OR
1920	Bevil Rudd, South Africa	49.6
1924	Eric Liddell, Great Britain	47.6 OR
1928	Ray Barbuti, United States	47.8
1932	William Carr, United States	46.2 WR
1936	Archie Williams, United States	46.5
1948	Arthur Wint, Jamaica	46.2
1952	George Rhoden, Jamaica	45.9
1956	Charles Jenkins, United States	46.7
1960	Otis Davis, United States	44.9 WR
1964	Michael Larrabee, United States	45.1
1968	Lee Evans, United States	43.86 WR
1972	Vincent Matthews, United States	44.66
1976	Alberto Juantorena, Cuba	44.26
1980	Viktor Markin, USSR	44.60
1984	Alonzo Babers, United States	44.27
1988	Steven Lewis, United States	43.87
1992	Quincy Watts, United States	43.50 (OR)

800 METERS

Year	Champion	Time
1896	Edwin Flack, Australia	2:11
1900	Alfred Tysoe, Great Britain	2:01.2
1904	James Lightbody, United States	1:56 OR
1906	Paul Pilgrim, United States	2:01.5
1908	Mel Sheppard, United States	1:52.8 WR
1912	James Meredith, United States	1:51.9 WR
1920	Albert Hill, Great Britain	1:53.4
1924	Douglas Lowe, Great Britain	1:52.4
1928	Douglas Lowe, Great Britain	1:51.8 OR
1932	Thomas Hampson, Great Britain	1:49.8 WR
1936	John Woodruff, United States	1:52.9
1948	Mal Whitfield, United States	1:49.2 OR
1952	Mal Whitfield, United States	1:49.2 EOR
1956	Thomas Courtney, United States	1:47.7 OR
1960	Peter Snell, New Zealand	1:46.3 OR
1964	Peter Snell, New Zealand	1:45.1 OR
1968	Ralph Doubell, Australia	1:44.3 EWR
1972	Dave Wottle, United States	1:45.9
1976	Alberto Juantorena, Cuba	1:43.50 OR
1980	Steve Ovett, Great Britain	1:45.40
1984	Joaquim Cruz, Brazil	1:43.00 OR
1988	Paul Ereng, Kenya	1:43.45
1992	William Tanui, Kenya	1:43.66

1500 METERS

Year	Champion	Time
1896	Edwin Flack, Australia	4:33.2
1900	Charles Bennett, Great Britain	4:06.2 WR
1904	James Lightbody, United States	4:05.4 WR
1906	James Lightbody, United States	4:12.0
1908	Mel Sheppard, United States	4:03.4 OR
1912	Arnold Jackson, Great Britain	3:56.8 OR
1920	Albert Hill, Great Britain	4:01.8
1924	Paavo Nurmi, Finland	3:53.6 OR
1928	Harry Larva, Finland	3:53.2 OR
1932	Luigi Beccali, Italy	3:51.2 OR
1936	Jack Lovelock, New Zealand	3:47.8 WR
1948	Henri Eriksson, Sweden	3:49.8
1952	Josef Barthel, Luxemburg	3:45.1 OR
1956	Ron Delany, Ireland	3:41.2 OR
1960	Herb Elliott, Australia	3:35.6 WR
1964	Peter Snell, New Zealand	3:38.1
1968	Kipchoge Keino, Kenya	3:34.9 OR
1972	Pekkha Vasala, Finland	3:36.3
1976	John Walker, New Zealand	3:39.17
1980	Sebastian Coe, Great Britain	3:38.4
1984	Sebastian Coe, Great Britain	3:32.53 OR
1988	Peter Rono, Kenya	3:35.96
1992	Fermin Cacho, Spain	3:40.12

5000 METERS

Year	Champion	Time
1912	Hannes Kolehmainen, Finland	14:36.6 WR
1920	Joseph Guillemot, France	14:55.6

1924	Paavo Nurmi, Finland	14:31.2 OR
1928	Villie Ritola, Finland	14:38
1932	Lauri Lehtinen, Finland	14:30 OR
1936	Gunnar Höckert, Finland	14:22.2 OR
1948	Gaston Reiff, Belgium	14:17.6 OR
1952	Emil Zatopek, Czechoslovakia	14:06.6 OR
1956	Vladimir Kuts, USSR	13:39.6 OR
1960	Murray Halberg, New Zealand	13:43.4
1964	Bob Schul, United States	13:48.8
1968	Mohamed Gammoudi, Tunisia	14:05.0
1972	Lasse Viren, Finland	13:26.4 OR
1976	Lasse Viren, Finland	13:24.76
1980	Miruts Yifter, Ethiopia	13:21.0
1984	Said Aouita, Morocco	13:05.59 OR
1988	John Ngugi, Kenya	13:11.70
1992	Dieter Baumann, Germany	13:12.52

10,000 METERS

1912	Hannes Kolehmainen, Finland	31:20.8
1920	Paavo Nurmi, Finland	31:45.8
1924	Villie Ritola, Finland	30:23.2 WR
1928	Paavo Nurmi, Finland	30:18.8 OR
1932	Janusz Kusocinski, Poland	30:11.4 OR
1936	Ilmari Salminen, Finland	30:15.4
1948	Emil Zatopek, Czechoslovakia	29:59.6 OR
1952	Emil Zatopek, Czechoslovakia	29:17.0 OR
1956	Vladimir Kuts, USSR	28:45.6 OR
1960	Pyotr Bolotnikov, USSR	28:32.2 OR
1964	Billy Mills, United States	28:24.4 OR
1968	Naftali Temu, Kenya	29:27.4
1972	Lasse Viren, Finland	27:38.4 WR
1976	Lasse Viren, Finland	27:40.38
1980	Miruts Yifter, Ethiopia	27:42.7
1984	Alberto Cova, Italy	27:47.54
1988	Brahim Boutaib, Morocco	27:21.46 OR
1992	Khalid Skah, Morocco	27:46.70

MARATHON

1896	Spiridon Louis, Greece	2:58:50
1900	Michel Theato, France	2:59:45
1904	Thomas Hicks, United States	3:28:53
1906	William Sherring, Canada	2:51:23.6
1908	John Hayes, United States	2:55:18.4 OR
1912	Kenneth McArthur, South Africa	2:36:54.8
1920	Hannes Kolehmainen, Finland	2:32:35.8 WB
1924	Albin Stenroos, Finland	2:41:22.6
1928	Boughera El Ouafi, France	2:32:57
1932	Juan Zabala, Argentina	2:31:36 OR
1936	Kijung Son, Japan (Korea)	2:29:19.2 OR
1948	Delfo Cabrera, Argentina	2:34:51.6
1952	Emil Zatopek, Czechoslovakia	2:23:03.2 OR
1956	Alain Mimoun, France	2:25
1960	Abebe Bikila, Ethiopia	2:15:16.2 WB
1964	Abebe Bikila, Ethiopia	2:12:11.2 WB
1968	Mamo Wolde, Ethiopia	2:20:26.4
1972	Frank Shorter, United States	2:12:19.8
1976	Waldemar Cierpinski, East Germany	2:09:55 OR
1980	Waldemar Cierpinski, East Germany	2:11:03.0
1984	Carlos Lopes, Portugal	2:09:21.0 OR
1988	Gelindo Bordin, Italy	2:10:32
1992	Hwang Young-Cho, S Korea	2:13.23

Note: Marathon distances: 1896, 1904—40,000 meters; 1900—40,260 meters; 1906—41,860 meters; 1912—40,200 meters; 1920—42,750 meters; 1908 and since 1924—42,195 meters (26 miles, 385 yards).

110-METER HURDLES

1896	Thomas Curtis, United States	17.6
1900	Alvin Kraenzlein, United States	15.4 OR
1904	Frederick Schule, United States	16.0
1906	Robert Leavitt, United States	16.2
1908	Forrest Smithson, United States	15.0 WR
1912	Frederick Kelly, United States	15.1
1920	Earl Thomson, Canada	14.8 WR
1924	Daniel Kinsey, United States	15
1928	Sydney Atkinson, South Africa	14.8
1932	George Saling, United States	14.6
1936	Forrest Towns, United States	14.2

1948	William Porter, United States	13.9 OR
1952	Harrison Dillard, United States	13.7 OR
1956	Lee Calhoun, United States	13.5 OR
1960	Lee Calhoun, United States	13.8
1964	Hayes Jones, United States	13.6
1968	Willie Davenport, United States	13.3 OR
1972	Rod Milburn, United States	13.24 EWR
1976	Guy Drut, France	13.30
1980	Thomas Munkelt, East Germany	13.39
1984	Roger Kingdom, United States	13.20 OR
1988	Roger Kingdom, United States	12.98 OR
1992	Mark McKoy, Canada	13.12

400-METER HURDLES

1900	John Walter Tewksbury, United States	57.6
1904	Harry Hillman, United States	53.0
1906	Not held	
1908	Charles Bacon, United States	55.0 WR
1912	Not held	
1920	Frank Loomis, United States	54.0 WR
1924	F. Morgan Taylor, United States	52.6
1928	David Burghley, Great Britain	53.4 OR
1932	Robert Tisdall, Ireland	51.7
1936	Glenn Hardin, United States	52.4
1948	Roy Cochran, United States	51.1 OR
1952	Charles Moore, United States	50.8 OR
1956	Glenn Davis, United States	50.1 EOR
1960	Glenn Davis, United States	49.3 EOR
1964	Rex Cawley, United States	49.6
1968	Dave Hemery, Great Britain	48.12 WR
1972	John Akii-Bua, Uganda	47.82 WR
1976	Edwin Moses, United States	47.64 WR
1980	Volker Beck, East Germany	48.70
1984	Edwin Moses, United States	47.75
1988	Andre Phillips, United States	47.19 OR
1992	Kevin Young, United States	46.78 WR

3000-METER STEEPLECHASE

1920	Percy Hodge, Great Britain	10:00.4 OR
1924	Villie Ritola, Finland	9:33.6 OR
1928	Toivo Loukola, Finland	9:21.8 WR
1932	Volmari Iso-Hollo, Finland*	10:33.4
1936	Volmari Iso-Hollo, Finland	9:03.8 WR
1948	Thore Sjöstrand, Sweden	9:04.6
1952	Horace Ashenfelter, United States	8:45.4 WR
1956	Chris Brasher, Great Britain	8:41.2 OR
1960	Zdzislaw Krzyszkowiak, Poland	8:34.2 OR
1964	Gaston Roelants, Belgium	8:30.8 OR
1968	Amos Biwott, Kenya	8:51
1972	Kipchoge Keino, Kenya	8:23.6 OR
1976	Anders Gärderud, Sweden	8:08.2 WR
1980	Bronislaw Malinowski, Poland	8:09.7
1984	Julius Korir, Kenya	8:11.8
1988	Julius Kariuki, Kenya	8:05.51 OR
1992	Mathew Birir, Kenya	8:08.84

*About 3450 meters; extra lap by error.

4 X 100-METER RELAY

1912	Great Britain	42.4 OR
1920	United States	42.2 WR
1924	United States	41.0 EWR
1928	United States	41.0 EWR
1932	United States	40.0 EWR
1936	United States	39.8 WR
1948	United States	40.6
1952	United States	40.1
1956	United States	39.5 WR
1960	West Germany	39.5 EWR
1964	United States	39.0 WR
1968	United States	38.2 WR
1972	United States	38.19 EWR
1976	United States	38.33
1980	USSR	38.26
1984	United States	37.83 WR
1988	USSR	38.19
1992	United States	37.40 WR

4 X 400-METER RELAY

1908	United States	3:29.4
1912	United States	3:16.6 WR
1920	Great Britain	3:22.2
1924	United States	3:16 WR
1928	United States	3:14.2 WR
1932	United States	3:08.2 WR
1936	Great Britain	3:09.0
1948	United States	3:10.4 WR
1952	Jamaica	3:03.9 WR
1956	United States	3:04.8
1960	United States	3:02.2 WR
1964	United States	3:00.7 WR
1968	United States	2:56.16 WR
1972	Kenya	2:59.8
1976	United States	2:58.65
1980	USSR	3:01.1
1984	United States	2:57.91
1988	United States	2:56.16 EWR
1992	United States	2:55.74

20-KILOMETER WALK

1956	Leonid Spirin, USSR	1:31:27.4
1960	Vladimir Golubnichiy, USSR	1:33:07.2
1964	Kenneth Mathews, Great Britain	1:29:34.0 OR
1968	Vladimir Golubnichiy, USSR	1:33:58.4
1972	Peter Frenkel, East Germany	1:26:42.4 OR
1976	Daniel Bautista, Mexico	1:24:40.6 OR
1980	Maurizio Damilano, Italy	1:23:35.5 OR
1984	Ernesto Canto, Mexico	1:23:13.0 OR
1988	Jozef Pribilinec, Czechoslovakia	1:19:57.0 OR
1992	Daniel Plaza, Spain	1:21:45

50-KILOMETER WALK

1932	Thomas Green, Great Britain	4:50:10
1936	Harold Whitlock, Great Britain	4:30:41.4 OR
1948	John Ljunggren, Sweden	4:41:52
1952	Giuseppe Dordoni, Italy	4:28:07.8 OR
1956	Norman Read, New Zealand	4:30:42.8
1960	Donald Thompson, Great Britain	4:25:30 OR
1964	Abdon Parnich, Italy	4:11:12.4 OR
1968	Christoph Höhne, East Germany	4:20:13.6
1972	Bernd Kannenberg, West Germany	3:56:11.6 OR
1980	Hartwig Gauder, East Germany	3:49:24.0 OR
1984	Raul Gonzalez, Mexico	3:47:26.0 OR
1988	Viacheslav Ivanenko, USSR	3:38:29.0 OR
1992	Andrey Perlov, Unified Team	3:50:13

HIGH JUMP

1896	Ellery Clark, United States	5 ft 11¼ in
1900	Irving Baxter, United States	6 ft 2¾ in OR
1904	Samuel Jones, United States	5 ft 11 in
1906	Cornelius Leahy, Great Britain/Ireland	5 ft 10 in
1908	Harry Porter, United States	6 ft 3 in OR
1912	Alma Richards, United States	6 ft 4 in OR
1920	Richmond Landon, United States	6 ft 4 in OR
1924	Harold Osborn, United States	6 ft 6 in OR
1928	Robert W. King, United States	6 ft 4½ in
1932	Duncan McNaughton, Canada	6 ft 5½ in
1936	Cornelius Johnson, United States	6 ft 8 in OR
1948	John L. Winter, Australia	6 ft 6 in
1952	Walter Davis, United States	6 ft 8½ in
1956	Charles Dumas, United States	6 ft 11½ in OR
1960	Robert Shavlakadze, USSR	7 ft 1 in OR
1964	Valery Brumel, USSR	7 ft 1¾ in OR
1968	Dick Fosbury, United States	7 ft 4¼ in OR
1972	Yuri Tarmak, USSR	7 ft 3¾ in
1976	Jacek Wszola, Poland	7 ft 4½ in OR
1980	Gerd Wessig, East Germany	7 ft 8¾ in WR
1984	Dietmar Mögenburg, West Germany	7 ft 8½ in
1988	Gennadiy Avdeyenko, USSR	7 ft 9¾ in OR
1992	Javier Sotomayor, Cuba	7ft 8 in

POLE VAULT

1896	William Hoyt, United States	10 ft 10 in
1900	Irving Baxter, United States	10 ft 10 in
1904	Charles Dvorak, United States	11 ft 5¾ in
1906	Fernand Gonder, France	11 ft 5¾ in
1908	Alfred Gilbert, United States	12 ft 2 in OR
	Edward Cooke, Jr, United States	
1912	Harry Babcock, United States	12 ft 11½ in OR
1920	Frank Foss, United States	13 ft 5 in WR
1924	Lee Barnes, United States	12 ft 11½ in
1928	Sabin Carr, United States	13 ft 9¼ in OR
1932	William Miller, United States	14 ft 1¾ in OR
1936	Earle Meadows, United States	14 ft 3¼ in OR
1948	Guinn Smith, United States	14 ft 1¼ in
1952	Robert Richards, United States	14 ft 11 in OR
1956	Robert Richards, United States	14 ft 11½ in OR
1960	Don Bragg, United States	15 ft 5 in OR
1964	Fred Hansen, United States	16 ft 8¾ in OR
1968	Bob Seagren, United States	17 ft 8½ in OR
1972	Wolfgang Nordwig, East Germany	18 ft ½ in OR
1976	Tadeusz Slusarski, Poland	18 ft ½ in EOR
1980	Wladyslaw Kozakiewicz, Poland	18 ft 11½ in WR
1984	Pierre Quinon, France	18 ft 10¼ in
1988	Sergei Bubka, USSR	19 ft 9¼ in OR
1992	Maksim Tarasov, Unified Team	19 ft ¼ in

LONG JUMP

1896	Ellery Clark, United States	20 ft 10 in
1900	Alvin Kraenzlein, United States	23 ft 6¾ in OR
1904	Meyer Prinstein, United States	24 ft 1 in OR
1906	Meyer Prinstein, United States	23 ft 7½ in
1908	Frank Irons, United States	24 ft 6½ in OR
1912	Albert Gutterson, United States	24 ft 11¼ in OR
1920	William Petersson, Sweden	23 ft 5½ in
1924	DeHart Hubbard, United States	24 ft 5 in
1928	Edward B. Hamm, United States	25 ft 4½ in OR
1932	Edward Gordon, United States	25 ft ¾ in
1936	Jesse Owens, United States	26 ft 5½ in OR
1948	William Steele, United States	25 ft 8 in
1952	Jerome Biffle, United States	24 ft 10 in
1956	Gregory Bell, United States	25 ft 8¼ in
1960	Ralph Boston, United States	26 ft 7¾ in OR
1964	Lynn Davies, Great Britain	26 ft 5¾ in
1968	Bob Beamon, United States	29 ft 2½ in WR
1972	Randy Williams, United States	27 ft ½ in
1976	Arnie Robinson, United States	27 ft 4¾ in
1980	Lutz Dombrowski, East Germany	28 ft ¼ in
1984	Carl Lewis, United States	28 ft ¼ in
1988	Carl Lewis, United States	28 ft 7½ in
1992	Carl Lewis, United States	28 ft 5½ in

TRIPLE JUMP

1896	James Connolly, United States	44 ft 11¾ in
1900	Meyer Prinstein, United States	47 ft 5¾ in OR
1904	Meyer Prinstein, United States	47 ft 1 in
1906	Peter O'Connor, Great Britain/Ireland	46 ft 2¼ in
1908	Timothy Ahearne, Great Britain/Ireland	48 ft 11¼ in OR
1912	Gustaf Lindblom, Sweden	48 ft 5¼ in
1920	Vilho Tuulos, Finland	47 ft 7 in
1924	Anthony Winter, Australia	50 ft 11¼ in WR
1928	Mikio Oda, Japan	49 ft 11 in
1932	Chuhei Nambu, Japan	51 ft 7 in WR
1936	Naoto Tajima, Japan	52 ft 6 in WR
1948	Arne Ahman, Sweden	50 ft 6¼ in
1952	Adhemar da Silva, Brazil	53 ft 2¾ in WR
1956	Adhemar da Silva, Brazil	53 ft 7¾ in WR
1960	Jozef Schmidt, Poland	55 ft 2 in
1964	Jozef Schmidt, Poland	55 ft 3½ in OR
1968	Viktor Saneyev, USSR	57 ft ¾ in WR
1972	Viktor Saneyev, USSR	56 ft 11¾ in
1976	Viktor Saneyev, USSR	56 ft 8¾ in
1980	Jaak Uudmae, USSR	56 ft 11¼ in
1984	Al Joyner, United States	56 ft 7½ in
1988	Khristo Markov, Bulgaria	57 ft 9½ in OR
1992	Mike Conley, United States	59 ft 7 ½ in

SHOT PUT

1896	Robert Garrett, United States	36 ft 9¾ in
1900	Richard Sheldon, United States	46 ft 3¼ in OR
1904	Ralph Rose, United States	48 ft 7 in WR
1906	Martin Sheridan, United States	40 ft 5¼ in
1908	Ralph Rose, United States	46 ft 7½ in
1912	Pat McDonald, United States	50 ft 4 in OR

BASKETBALL

MEN

1936
Final: United States 19, Canada 8
United States: Ralph Bishop, Joe Fortenberry, Carl Knowles, Jack Ragland, Carl Shy, William Wheatley, Francis Johnson, Samuel Balter, John Gibbons, Frank Lubin, Arthur Mollner, Donald Piper, Duane Swanson, Willard Schmidt

1948
Final: United States 65, France 21
United States: Cliff Barker, Don Barksdale, Ralph Beard, Lewis Beck, Vince Boryla, Gordon Carpenter, Alex Groza, Wallace Jones, Bob Kurland, Ray Lumpp, Robert Pitts, Jesse Renick, Bob Robinson, Ken Rollins

1952
Final: United States 36, USSR 25
United States: Charles Hoag, Bill Hougland, Melvin Dean Kelley, Bob Kenney, Clyde Lovellette, Marcus Freiberger, Victor Wayne Glasgow, Frank McCabe, Daniel Pippen, Howard Williams, Ronald Bontemps, Bob Kurland, William Lienhard, John Keller

1956
Final: United States 89, USSR 55
United States: Carl Cain, Bill Hougland, K. C. Jones, Bill Russell, James Walsh, William Evans, Burdette Haldorson, Ron Tomsic, Dick Boushka, Gilbert Ford, Bob Jeangerard, Charles Darling

1960
Final: United States 90, Brazil 63
United States: Jay Arnette, Walt Bellamy, Bob Boozer, Terry Dischinger, Jerry Lucas, Oscar Robertson, Adrian Smith, Burdette Haldorson, Darrall Imhoff, Allen Kelley, Lester Lane, Jerry West

1964
Final: United States 73, USSR 59
United States: Jim Barnes, Bill Bradley, Larry Brown, Joe Caldwell, Mel Counts, Richard Davies, Walt Hazzard, Lucius Jackson, John McCaffrey, Jeff Mullins, Jerry Shipp, George Wilson

1968
Final: United States 65, Yugoslavia 50
United States: John Clawson, Ken Spain, Jo-Jo White, Michael Barrett, Spencer Haywood, Charles Scott, William Hosket, Calvin Fowler, Michael Silliman, Glynn Saulters, James King, Donald Dee

1972
Final: USSR 51, United States 50
United States: Kenneth Davis, Doug Collins, Thomas Henderson, Mike Bantom, Bobby Jones, Dwight Jones, James Forbes, James Brewer, Tom Burleson, Tom McMillen, Kevin Joyce, Ed Ratleff

1976
Final: United States 95, Yugoslavia 74
United States: Phil Ford, Steve Sheppard, Adrian Dantley, Walter Davis, Quinn Buckner, Ernie Grunfield, Kenny Carr, Scott May, Michel Armstrong, Tom La Garde, Phil Hubbard, Mitch Kupchak

1980
Final: Yugoslavia 86, Italy 77
U.S. participated in boycott.

1984
Final: United States 96, Spain 65
United States: Steve Alford, Leon Wood, Patrick Ewing, Vern Fleming, Alvin Robertson, Michael Jordan, Joe Kleine, Jon Koncak, Wayman Tisdale, Chris Mullin, Sam Perkins, Jeff Turner

1988
Final: USSR 76, Yugoslavia 63
United States (3rd): Mitch Richmond, Charles E. Smith, IV, Vernell Coles, Hersey Hawkins, Jeff Grayer, Charles D. Smith, Willie Anderson, Stacey Augmon, Dan Majerle, Danny Manning, J. R. Reid, David Robinson

1992
Final: United States 117, Croatia 85
United States: David Robinson, Christian Laettner, Patrick Ewing, Larry Bird, Scottie Pippen, Michael Jordan, Clyde Drexler, Karl Malone, John Stockton, Chris Mullin, Charles Barkley, Earvin Johnson

WOMEN

1976
Gold USSR; Silver, United States*
United States: Cindy Brogdon, Susan Rojcewicz, Ann Meyers, Lusia Harris, Nancy Dunkle, Charlotte Lewis, Nancy Lieberman, Gail Marquis, Patricia Roberts, Mary Anne O'Connor, Patricia Head, Julienne Simpson

*In 1976 the women played a round-robin tournament, with the gold medal going to the team with the best record. The USSR won with a 5-0 record, and the USA, with a 3-2 record, was given the silver by virtue of a 95-79 victory over Bulgaria, which was also 3-2.

1980
Final: USSR 104, Bulgaria 73
U.S. participated in boycott.

1988
Final: United States 77, Yugoslavia 70
United States: Teresa Edwards, Mary Ethridge, Cynthia Brown, Anne Donovan, Teresa Weatherspoon, Bridgette Gordon, Victoria Bullett, Andrea Lloyd, Katrina McClain, Jennifer Gillom, Cynthia Cooper, Suzanne McConnell

1992
Final: Unified Team 76, China 66
United States (3rd): Teresa Edwards, Teresa Weatherspoon, Victoria Bullett, Katrina McClain, Cynthia Cooper, Suzanne McConnell, Daedra Charles, Clarissa Davis, Tammy Jackson, Vickie Orr, Carolyn Jones, Medina Dixon

BOXING

LIGHT FLYWEIGHT (106 LB)
1968	Francisco Rodriguez, Venezuela
1972	Gyorgy Gedo, Hungary
1976	Jorge Hernandez, Cuba
1980	Shamil Sabyrov, USSR
1984	Paul Gonzalez, United States
1988	Ivailo Hristov, Bulgaria
1992	Rogelia Marcelo, Cuba

FLYWEIGHT (112 LB)
1904	George Finnegan, United States
1906-1912	Not held
1920	Frank Di Gennara, United States
1924	Fidel LaBarba, United States
1928	Antal Kocsis, Hungary
1932	Istvan Enekes, Hungary
1936	Willi Kaiser, Germany
1948	Pascual Perez, Argentina
1952	Nathan Brooks, United States
1956	Terence Spinks, Great Britain
1960	Gyula Torok, Hungary
1964	Fernando Atzori, Italy
1968	Ricardo Delgado, Mexico
1972	Georgi Kostadinov, Bulgaria
1976	Leo Randolph, United States
1980	Peter Lessov, Bulgaria
1984	Steve McCrory, United States
1988	Kim Kwang Sun, South Korea
1992	Su Choi Chol, North Korea

BANTAMWEIGHT (119 LB)
1904	Oliver Kirk, United States
1906	Not held
1908	A. Henry Thomas, Great Britain

1912	Not held
1920	Clarence Walker, South Africa
1924	William Smith, South Africa
1928	Vittorio Tamagnini, Italy
1932	Horace Gwynne, Canada
1936	Ulderico Sergo, Italy
1948	Tibor Csik, Hungary
1952	Pentti Hamalainen, Finland
1956	Wolfgang Behrendt, East Germany
1960	Oleg Grigoryev, USSR
1964	Takao Sakurai, Japan
1968	Valery Sokolov, USSR
1972	Orlando Martinez, Cuba
1976	Yong Jo Gu, North Korea
1980	Juan Hernandez, Cuba
1984	Maurizio Stecca, Italy
1988	Kennedy McKinney, United States
1992	Joel Casamayor, Cuba

FEATHERWEIGHT (125 LB)

1904	Oliver Kirk, United States
1906	Not held
1908	Richard Gunn, Great Britain
1912	Not held
1920	Paul Fritsch, France
1924	John Fields, United States
1928	Lambertus van Klaveren, Netherlands
1932	Carmelo Robledo, Argentina
1936	Oscar Casanovas, Argentina
1948	Ernesto Formenti, Italy
1952	Jan Zachara, Czechoslovakia
1956	Vladimir Safronov, USSR
1960	Francesco Musso, Italy
1964	Stanislav Stephashkin, USSR
1968	Antonio Roldan, Mexico
1972	Boris Kousnetsov, USSR
1976	Angel Herrera, Cuba
1980	Rudi Fink, East Germany
1984	Meldrick Taylor, United States
1988	Giovanni Parisi, Italy
1992	Andreas Tews, Germany

LIGHTWEIGHT (132 LB)

1904	Harry Spanger, United States
1906	Not held
1908	Frederick Grace, Great Britain
1912	Not held
1920	Samuel Mosberg, United States
1924	Hans Nielsen, Denmark
1928	Carlo Orlandi, Italy
1932	Lawrence Stevens, South Africa
1936	Imre Harangi, Hungary
1948	Gerald Dreyer, South Africa
1952	Aureliano Bolognesi, Italy
1956	Richard McTaggart, Great Britain
1960	Kazimierz Pazdzior, Poland
1964	Jozef Grudzien, Poland
1968	Ronald Harris, United States
1972	Jan Szczepanski, Poland
1976	Howard Davis, United States
1980	Angel Herrera, Cuba
1984	Pernell Whitaker, United States
1988	Andreas Zuelow, East Germany
1992	Oscar De La Hoya, United States

LIGHT WELTERWEIGHT (139 LB)

1952	Charles Adkins, United States
1956	Vladimir Yengibaryan, USSR
1960	Bohumil Nemecek, Czechoslovakia
1964	Jerzy Kulej, Poland
1968	Jerzy Kulej, Poland
1972	Ray Seales, United States
1976	Ray Leonard, United States
1980	Patrizio Oliva, Italy
1984	Jerry Page, United States
1988	Viatcheslav Janovski, USSR
1992	Hector Vinent, Cuba

WELTERWEIGHT (147 LB)

1904	Albert Young, United States
1906-1912	Not held
1920	Albert Schneider, Canada
1924	Jean Delarge, Belgium
1928	Edward Morgan, New Zealand
1932	Edward Flynn, United States
1936	Sten Suvio, Finland
1948	Julius Torma, Czechoslovakia
1952	Zygmunt Chychla, Poland
1956	Nicolae Linca, Romania
1960	Giovanni Benvenuti, Italy
1964	Marian Kasprzyk, Poland
1968	Manfred Wolke, East Germany
1972	Emilio Correa, Cuba
1976	Jochen Bachfeld, East Germany
1980	Andres Aldama, Cuba
1984	Mark Breland, United States
1988	Robert Wangila, Kenya
1992	Michael Carruth, Ireland

LIGHT MIDDLEWEIGHT (156 LB)

1952	Laszlo Papp, Hungary
1956	Laszlo Papp, Hungary
1960	Wilbert McClure, United States
1964	Boris Lagutin, USSR
1968	Boris Lagutin, USSR
1972	Dieter Kottysch, West Germany
1976	Jerzy Rybicki, Poland
1980	Armando Martinez, Cuba
1984	Frank Tate, United States
1988	Park Si-Hun, South Korea
1992	Jaun Lemus, Cuba

MIDDLEWEIGHT (165 LB)

1904	Charles Mayer, United States
1908	John Douglas, Great Britain
1912	Not held
1920	Harry Mallin, Great Britain
1924	Harry Mallin, Great Britain
1928	Piero Toscani, Italy
1932	Carmen Barth, United States
1936	Jean Despeaux, France
1948	Laszlo Papp, Hungary
1952	Floyd Patterson, United States
1956	Gennady Schatkov, USSR
1960	Edward Crook, United States
1964	Valery Popenchenko, USSR
1968	Christopher Finnegan, Great Britain
1972	Vyacheslav Lemechev, USSR
1976	Michael Spinks, United States
1980	Jose Gomez, Cuba
1984	Shin Joon Sup, South Korea
1988	Henry Maske, East Germany
1992	Ariel Hernandez, Cuba

LIGHT HEAVYWEIGHT (178 LB)

1920	Edward Eagan, United States
1924	Harry Mitchell, Great Britain
1928	Victor Avendano, Argentina
1932	David Carstens, South Africa
1936	Roger Michelot, France
1948	George Hunter, South Africa
1952	Norvel Lee, United States
1956	James Boyd, United States
1960	Cassius Clay, United States
1964	Cosimo Pinto, Italy
1968	Dan Poznyak, USSR
1972	Mate Parlov, Yugoslavia
1976	Leon Spinks, United States
1980	Slobodan Kacer, Yugoslavia
1984	Anton Josipovic, Yugoslavia
1988	Andrew Maynard, United States
1992	Torsten May, Germany

HEAVYWEIGHT (OVER 201 LB)

1904	Samuel Berger, United States

1906	Not held
1908	Albert Oldham, Great Britain
1912	Not held
1920	Ronald Rawson, Great Britain
1924	Otto von Porat, Norway
1928	Arturo Rodriguez Jurado, Argentina
1932	Santiago Lovell, Argentina
1936	Herbert Runge, Germany
1948	Rafael Inglesias, Argentina
1952	H. Edward Sanders, United States
1956	T. Peter Rademacher, United States
1960	Franco De Piccoli, Italy
1964	Joe Frazier, United States
1968	George Foreman, United States
1972	Teofilo Stevenson, Cuba
1976	Teofilo Stevenson, Cuba
1980	Teofilo Stevenson, Cuba

HEAVYWEIGHT (201* LB)

1984	Henry Tillman, United States
1988	Ray Mercer, United States
1992	Felix Savon, Cuba

SUPER HEAVYWEIGHT (UNLIMITED)

1984	Tyrell Biggs, United States
1988	Lennox Lewis, Canada
1992	Roberto Balado, Cuba

*Until 1984 the heavyweight division was unlimited. With the addition of the super heavyweight division, a limit of 201 pounds was imposed.

SWIMMING

MEN

50-METER FREESTYLE

1904	Zoltan Halmay, Hungary (50 yds)	28.0
1988	Matt Biondi, United States	22.14 WR
1992	Aleksandr Popov, Unified Team	22.30

100-METER FREESTYLE

1896	Alfred Hajos, Hungary	1:22.2 OR
1904	Zoltan Halmay, Hungary (100 yds)	1:02.8
1906	Charles Daniels, United States	1:13.4
1908	Charles Daniels, United States	1:05.6 WR
1912	Duke Kahanamoku, United States	1:03.4
1920	Duke Kahanamoku, United States	1:00.4 WR
1924	John Weissmuller, United States	59.0 OR
1928	John Weissmuller, United States	58.6 OR
1932	Yasuji Miyazaki, Japan	58.2
1936	Ferenc Csik, Hungary	57.6
1948	Wally Ris, United States	57.3 OR
1952	Clarke Scholes, United States	57.4
1956	Jon Henricks, Australia	55.4 OR
1960	John Devitt, Australia	55.2 OR
1964	Don Schollander, United States	53.4 WR
1968	Mike Wenden, Australia	52.2 WR
1972	Mark Spitz, United States	51.22 WR
1976	Jim Montgomery, United States	49.99 WR
1980	Jörg Woithe, East Germany	50.40
1984	Rowdy Gaines, United States	49.80 OR
1988	Matt Biondi, United States	48.63 OR
1992	Aleksandr Popov, Unified Team	49.02

200-METER FREESTYLE

1900	Frederick Lane, Australia	2:25.2 OR
1904	Charles Daniels, United States	2:44.2
1906	Not held 1906-1964	
1968	Michael Wenden, Australia	1:55.2 OR
1972	Mark Spitz, United States	1:52.78 WR
1976	Bruce Furniss, United States	1:50.29 WR
1980	Sergei Kopliakov, USSR	1:49.81 OR
1984	Michael Gross, West Germany	1:47.44 WR
1988	Duncan Armstrong, Australia	1:47.25 WR
1992	Evgueni Sadovyi, Unified Team	1:46.70

400-METER FREESTYLE

1896	Paul Neumann, Austria (500 yds)	8:12.6
1904	Charles Daniels, U.S. (440 yds)	6:16.2
1906	Otto Scheff, Austria (440 yds)	6:23.8
1908	Henry Taylor, Great Britain	5:36.8
1912	George Hodgson, Canada	5:24.4
1920	Norman Ross, United States	5:26.8
1924	John Weissmuller, United States	5:04.2 OR
1928	Albert Zorilla, Argentina	5:01.6 OR
1932	Buster Crabbe, United States	4:48.4 OR
1936	Jack Medica, United States	4:44.5 OR
1948	William Smith, United States	4:41.0 OR
1952	Jean Boiteux, France	4:30.7 OR
1956	Murray Rose, Australia	4:27.3 OR
1960	Murray Rose, Australia	4:18.3 OR
1964	Don Schollander, United States	4:12.2 WR
1968	Mike Burton, United States	4:09.0 OR
1972	Brad Cooper, Australia	4:00.27 OR
1976	Brian Goodell, United States	3:51.93 WR
1980	Vladimir Salnikov, USSR	3:51.31 OR
1984	George DiCarlo, United States	3:51.23 OR
1988	Uwe Dassler, East Germany	3:46.95 WR
1992	Evgueni Sadovyi, Unified Team	3:45.0

1500-METER FREESTYLE

1908	Henry Taylor, Great Britain	22:48.4 WR
1912	George Hodgson, Canada	22:00.0 WR
1920	Norman Ross, United States	22:23.2
1924	Andrew Charlton, Australia	20:06.6 WR
1928	Arne Borg, Sweden	19:51.8 OR
1932	Kusuo Kitamura, Japan	19:12.4 OR
1936	Noboru Terada, Japan	19:13.7
1948	James McLane, United States	19:18.5
1952	Ford Konno, United States	18:30.3 OR
1956	Murray Rose, Australia	17:58.9
1960	John Konrads, Australia	17:19.6 OR
1964	Robert Windle, Australia	17:01.7 OR
1968	Mike Burton, United States	16:38.9 OR
1972	Mike Burton, United States	15:52.58 OR
1976	Brian Goodell, United States	15:02.40 WR
1980	Vladimir Salnikov, USSR	14:58.27 WR
1984	Michael O'Brien, United States	15:05.20
1988	Vladimir Salnikov, USSR	15:00.40
1992	Kieren Perkins, Australia	14:43.48 WR

100-METER BACKSTROKE

1904	Walter Brack, Germany (100 yds)	1:16.8
1908	Arno Bieberstein, Germany	1:24.6 WR
1912	Harry Hebner, United States	1:21.2
1920	Warren Kealoha, United States	1:15.2
1924	Warren Kealoha, United States	1:13.2 OR
1928	George Kojac, United States	1:08.2 WR
1932	Masaji Kiyokawa, Japan	1:08.6
1936	Adolph Kiefer, United States	1:05.9 OR
1948	Allen Stack, United States	1:06.4
1952	Yoshi Oyakawa, United States	1:05.4 OR
1956	David Thiele, Australia	1:02.2 OR
1960	David Thiele, Australia	1:01.9 OR
1964	Not held	
1968	Roland Matthes, East Germany	58.7 OR
1972	Roland Matthes, East Germany	56.58 OR
1976	John Naber, United States	55.49 WR
1980	Bengt Baron, Sweden	56.33
1984	Rick Carey, United States	55.79
1988	Daichi Suzuki, Japan	55.05
1992	Mark Tewksbury, Canada	53.98 WR

200-METER BACKSTROKE

1900	Ernst Hoppenberg, Germany	2:47.0
1904	Not held 1904-1960	
1964	Jed Graef, United States	2:10.3 WR
1968	Roland Matthes, East Germany	2:09.6 OR
1972	Roland Matthes, East Germany	2:02.82 EWR
1976	John Naber, United States	1:59.19 WR

1980	Sandor Wladar, Hungary	2:01.93
1984	Rick Carey, United States	2:00.23
1988	Igor Polianski, USSR	1:59.37
1992	Martin Zubero-Lopez, Spain	1:58.47 OR

100-METER BREASTSTROKE

1968	Don McKenzie, United States	1:07.7 OR
1972	Nobutaka Taguchi, Japan	1:04.94 WR
1976	John Hencken, United States	1:03.11 WR
1980	Duncan Goodhew, Great Britain	1:03.44
1984	Steve Lundquist, United States	1:01.65 WR
1988	Adrian Moorhouse, Great Britain	1:02.04
1992	Nelson Diebel, United States	1:01.50 OR

200-METER BREASTSTROKE

1908	Frederick Holman, Great Britain	3:09.2 WR
1912	Walter Bathe, Germany	3:01.8 OR
1920	Haken Malmroth, Sweden	3:04.4
1924	Robert Skelton, United States	2:56.6
1928	Yoshiyuki Tsuruta, Japan	2:48.8 OR
1932	Yoshiyuki Tsuruta, Japan	2:45.4
1936	Tetsuo Hamuro, Japan	2:41.5 OR
1948	Joseph Verdeur, United States	2:39.3 OR
1952	John Davies, Australia	2:34.4 OR
1956	Masura Furukawa, Japan	2:34.7 OR
1960	William Mulliken, United States	2:37.4
1964	Ian O'Brien, Australia	2:27.8 WR
1968	Felipe Munoz, Mexico	2:28.7
1972	John Hencken, United States	2:21.55 WR
1976	David Wilkie, Great Britain	2:15.11 WR
1980	Robertas Zhulpa, USSR	2:15.85
1984	Victor Davis, Canada	2:13.34 WR
1988	Jozsef Szabo, Hungary	2:13.52
1992	Mike Barrowman, United States	2:10.16

100-METER BUTTERFLY

1968	Doug Russell, United States	55.9 OR
1972	Mark Spitz, United States	54.27 WR
1976	Matt Vogel, United States	54.35
1980	Pär Arvidsson, Sweden	54.92
1984	Michael Gross, West Germany	53.08 WR
1988	Anthony Nesty, Suriname	53.00 OR
1992	Pablo Morales, United States	53.32

200-METER BUTTERFLY

1956	William Yorzyk, United States	2:19.3 OR
1960	Michael Troy, United States	2:12.8 WR
1964	Kevin Berry, Australia	2:06.6 WR
1968	Carl Robie, United States	2:08.7
1972	Mark Spitz, United States	2:00.70 WR
1976	Mike Bruner, United States	1:59.23 WR
1980	Sergei Fesenko, USSR	1:59.76
1984	Jon Sieben, Australia	1:57.04 WR
1988	Michael Gross, West Germany	1:56.94 OR
1992	Melvin Stewart, United States	1:56.26

200-METER INDIVIDUAL MEDLEY

1968	Charles Hickcox, United States	2:12.0 OR
1972	Gunnar Larsson, Sweden	2:07.17 WR
1984	Alex Baumann, Canada	2:01.42 WR
1988	Tamas Darnyi, Hungary	2:00.17 WR
1992	Tamas Darnyi, Hungary	2:00.76

400-METER INDIVIDUAL MEDLEY

1964	Richard Roth, United States	4:45.4 WR
1968	Charles Hickcox, United States	4:48.4
1972	Gunnar Larsson, Sweden	4:31.98 WR
1976	Rod Strachan, United States	4:23.68 WR
1980	Aleksandr Sidorenko, USSR	4:22.89 OR
1984	Alex Baumann, Canada	4:17.41 WR
1988	Tamas Darnyi, Hungary	4:14.75 WR
1992	Tamas Darnyi, Hungary	4:14.23 OR

4 X 100-METER MEDLEY RELAY

1960	United States	4:05.4 WR
1964	United States	3:58.4 WR
1968	United States	3:54.9 WR

1972	United States	3:48.16 WR
1976	United States	3:42.22 WR
1980	Australia	3:45.70
1984	United States	3:39.30 WR
1988	United States	3:36.93 WR
1992	United States	3:36.93

4 X 400-METER FREESTYLE RELAY

1964	United States	3:32.2 WR
1968	United States	3:31.7 WR
1972	United States	3:26.42 WR
1976-1980		Not held
1984	United States	3:19.03 WR
1988	United States	3:16.53 WR
1992	United States	3:16.74

4 X 200-METER FREESTYLE RELAY

1906	Hungary (1000 m)	16:52.4
1908	Great Britain	10:55.6
1912	Australia/New Zealand	10:11.6 WR
1920	United States	10:04.4 WR
1924	United States	9:53.4 WR
1928	United States	9:36.2 WR
1932	Japan	8:58.4 WR
1936	Japan	8:51.5 WR
1948	United States	8:46.0 WR
1952	United States	8:31.1 OR
1956	Australia	8:23.6 WR
1960	United States	8:10.2 WR
1964	United States	7:52.1 WR
1968	United States	7:52.33
1972	United States	7:35.78 WR
1976	United States	7:23.22 WR
1980	USSR	7:23.50
1984	United States	7:15.69 WR
1988	United States	7:12.51 WR
1992	Unified Team	7:11.95 WR

WOMEN

50-METER FREESTYLE

1988	Kristin Otto, East Germany	25.49 OR
1992	Yang Wenyi, China	24.79 WR

100-METER FREESTYLE

1912	Fanny Durack, Australia	1:22.2
1920	Ethelda Bleibtrey, United States	1:13.6 WR
1924	Ethel Lackie, United States	1:12.4
1928	Albina Osipowich, United States	1:11.0 OR
1932	Helene Madison, United States	1:06.8 OR
1936	Hendrika Mastenbroek, Netherlands	1:05.9 OR
1948	Greta Andersen, Denmark	1:06.3
1952	Katalin Szöke, Hungary	1:06.8
1956	Dawn Fraser, Australia	1:02.0 WR
1960	Dawn Fraser, Australia	1:01.2 OR
1964	Dawn Fraser, Australia	59.5 OR
1968	Jan Henne, United States	1:00.0
1972	Sandra Neilson, United States	58.59 OR
1976	Kornelia Ender, East Germany	55.65 WR
1980	Barbara Krause, East Germany	54.79 WR
1984	Carrie Steinseifer, United States	55.92
	Nancy Hogshead, United States	55.92
1988	Kristin Otto, East Germany	54.93
1992	Zhuang Yong, China	54.64 OR

200-METER FREESTYLE

1968	Debbie Meyer, United States	2:10.5 OR
1972	Shane Gould, Australia	2:03.56 WR
1976	Kornelia Ender, East Germany	1:59.26 WR
1980	Barbara Krause, East Germany	1:58.33 OR
1984	Mary Wayte, United States	1:59.23
1988	Heike Friedrich, East Germany	1:57.65 OR
1992	Nicole Haislett, United States	1:57.90

400-METER FREESTYLE

1924	Martha Norelius, United States	6:02.2 OR
1928	Martha Norelius, United States	5:42.8 WR
1932	Helene Madison, United States	5:28.5 WR
1936	Hendrika Mastenbroek, Netherlands	5:26.4 OR
1948	Ann Curtis, United States	5:17.8 OR
1952	Valeria Gyenge, Hungary	5:12.1 OR
1956	Lorraine Crapp, Australia	4:54.6 OR
1960	Chris von Saltza, United States	4:50.6 OR
1964	Virginia Duenkel, United States	4:43.3 OR
1968	Debbie Meyer, United States	4:31.8 OR
1972	Shane Gould, Australia	4:19.44 WR
1976	Petra Thümer, East Germany	4:09.89 WR
1980	Ines Diers, East Germany	4:08.76 WR
1984	Tiffany Cohen, United States	4:07.10 OR
1988	Janet Evans, United States	4:03.85 WR
1992	Dagmar Hase, Germany	4:07.18

800-METER FREESTYLE

1968	Debbie Meyer, United States	9:24.0 OR
1972	Keena Rothhammer, United States	8:53.68 WR
1976	Petra Thümer, East Germany	8:37.14 WR
1980	Michelle Ford, Australia	8:28.90 OR
1984	Tiffany Cohen, United States	8:24.95 OR
1988	Janet Evans, United States	8:20.20 OR
1992	Janet Evans, United States	8:25.52

100-METER BACKSTROKE

1924	Sybil Bauer, United States	1:23.2 OR
1928	Marie Braun, Netherlands	1:22.0
1932	Eleanor Holm, United States	1:19.4
1936	Dina Senff, Netherlands	1:18.9
1948	Karen Harup, Denmark	1:14.4 OR
1952	Joan Harrison, South Africa	1:14.3
1956	Judy Grinham, Great Britain	1:12.9 OR
1960	Lynn Burke, United States	1:09.3 OR
1964	Cathy Ferguson, United States	1:07.7 WR
1968	Kaye Hall, United States	1:06.2 WR
1972	Melissa Belote, United States	1:05.78 OR
1976	Ulrike Richter, East Germany	1:01.83 OR
1980	Rica Reinisch, East Germany	1:00.86 WR
1984	Theresa Andrews, United States	1:02.55
1988	Kristin Otto, East Germany	1:00.89
1992	Krisztina Egerszegi, Hungary	1:00.68 OR

200-METER BACKSTROKE

1968	Pokey Watson, United States	2:24.8 OR
1972	Melissa Belote, United States	2:19.19 WR
1976	Ulrike Richter, East Germany	2:13.43 OR
1980	Rica Reinisch, East Germany	2:11.77 WR
1984	Jolanda De Rover, Netherlands	2:12.38
1988	Krisztina Egerszegi, Hungary	2:09.29 OR
1992	Krisztina Egerszegi, Hungary	2:07.06

100-METER BREASTSTROKE

1968	Djurdjica Bjedov, Yugoslavia	1:15.8 OR
1972	Catherine Carr, United States	1:13.58 WR
1976	Hannelore Anke, East Germany	1:11.16
1980	Ute Geweniger, East Germany	1:10.22
1984	Petra Van Staveren, Netherlands	1:09.88 OR
1988	Tania Dangalakova, Bulgaria	1:07.95 OR
1992	Elena Roudkovskaia, Unified Team	1:08.00

200-METER BREASTSTROKE

1924	Lucy Morton, Great Britain	3:33.2 OR
1928	Hilde Schrader, Germany	3:12.6
1932	Clare Dennis, Australia	3:06.3 OR
1936	Hideko Maehata, Japan	3:03.6
1948	Petronella Van Vliet, Netherlands	2:57.2
1952	Eva Szekely, Hungary	2:51.7 OR
1956	Ursula Happe, West Germany	2:53.1 OR
1960	Anita Lonsbrough, Great Britain	2:49.5 WR
1964	Galina Prozumenshikova, USSR	2:46.4 OR
1968	Sharon Wichman, United States	2:44.4 OR
1972	Beverly Whitfield, Australia	2:41.71 OR
1976	Marina Koshevaia, USSR	2:33.35 WR
1980	Lina Kaciusyte, USSR	2:29.54 OR

1984	Anne Ottenbrite, Canada	2:30.38
1988	Silke Hoerner, East Germany	2:26.71 WR
1992	Kyoko Iwasaki, Japan	2:26.65 OR

100-METER BUTTERFLY

1956	Shelley Mann, United States	1:11.0 OR
1960	Carolyn Schuler, United States	1:09.5 OR
1964	Sharon Stouder, United States	1:04.7 WR
1968	Lynn McClements, Australia	1:05.5
1972	Mayumi Aoki, Japan	1:03.34 WR
1976	Kornelia Ender, East Germany	1:00.13 EWR
1980	Caren Metschuck, East Germany	1:00.42
1984	Mary T. Meagher, United States	59.26
1988	Kristin Otto, East Germany	59.00 OR
1992	Qian Hong, China	58.62 WR

200-METER BUTTERFLY

1968	Ada Kok, Netherlands	2:24.7 OR
1972	Karen Moe, United States	2:15.57 WR
1976	Andrea Pollack, East Germany	2:11.41 OR
1980	Ines Geissler, East Germany	2:10.44 OR
1984	Mary T. Meagher, United States	2:06.90 OR
1988	Kathleen Nord, East Germany	2:09.51
1992	Summer Sanders, United States	2:08.67

200-METER INDIVIDUAL MEDLEY

1968	Claudia Kolb, United States	2:24.7 OR
1972	Shane Gould, Australia	2:23.07 WR
1976	Not held 1976-1980	
1984	Tracy Caulkins, United States	2:12.64 OR
1988	Daniela Hunger, East Germany	2:12.59 OR
1992	Lin Li, China	2:11.65 WR

400-METER INDIVIDUAL MEDLEY

1964	Donna de Varona, United States	5:18.7 OR
1968	Claudia Kolb, United States	5:08.5 OR
1972	Gail Neall, Australia	5:02.97 WR
1976	Ulrike Tauber, East Germany	4:42.77 WR
1980	Petra Schneider, East Germany	4:36.29 WR
1984	Tracy Caulkins, United States	4:39.24
1988	Janet Evans, United States	4:37.76
1992	Krisztina Egerszegi, Hungary	4:36.54

4 X 100-METER MEDLEY RELAY

1960	United States	4:41.1 WR
1964	United States	4:33.9 WR
1968	United States	4:28.3 OR
1972	United States	4:20.75 WR
1976	East Germany	4:07.95 WR
1980	East Germany	4:06.67 WR
1984	United States	4:08.34
1988	East Germany	4:03.74 OR
1992	United States	4:02.54 WR

4 X 100-METER FREESTYLE RELAY

1912	Great Britain	5:52.8 WR
1920	United States	5:11.6 WR
1924	United States	4:58.8 WR
1928	United States	4:47.6 WR
1932	United States	4:38.0 WR
1936	Netherlands	4:36.0 OR
1948	United States	4:29.2 WR
1952	Hungary	4:24.4 WR
1956	Australia	4:17.1 WR
1960	United States	4:08.9 WR
1964	United States	4:03.8 WR
1968	United States	4:02.5 OR
1972	United States	3:55.19 WR
1976	United States	3:44.82 WR
1980	East Germany	3:42.71 WR
1984	United States	3:43.43
1988	East Germany	3:40.63 OR
1992	United States	3:39.46 WR

DIVING

MEN

SPRINGBOARD

		PTS
1908	Albert Zürner, Germany	85.5
1912	Paul Günther, Germany	79.23
1920	Louis Kuehn, United States	675.40
1924	Albert White, United States	97.46
1928	Pete DesJardins, United States	185.04
1932	Michael Galitzen, United States	161.38
1936	Richard Degener, United States	163.57
1948	Bruce Harlan, United States	163.64
1952	David Browning, United States	205.29
1956	Robert Clotworthy, United States	159.56
1960	Gary Tobian, United States	170.00
1964	Kenneth Sitzberger, United States	159.90
1968	Bernie Wrightson, United States	170.15
1972	Vladimir Vasin, USSR	594.09
1976	Phil Boggs, United States	619.05
1980	Aleksandr Portnov, USSR	905.02
1984	Greg Louganis, United States	754.41
1988	Greg Louganis, United States	730.80
1992	Mark Lenzi, United States	676.53

PLATFORM

		PTS
1904	George Sheldon, United States	12.66
1906	Gottlob Walz, Germany	156.0
1908	Hjalmar Johansson, Sweden	83.75
1912	Erik Adlerz, Sweden	73.94
1920	Clarence Pinkston, United States	100.67
1924	Albert White, United States	97.46
1928	Pete DesJardins, United States	98.74
1932	Harold Smith, United States	124.80
1936	Marshall Wayne, United States	113.58
1948	Sammy Lee, United States	130.05
1952	Sammy Lee, United States	156.28
1956	Joaquin Capilla, Mexico	152.44
1960	Robert Webster, United States	165.56
1964	Robert Webster, United States	148.58
1968	Klaus Dibiasi, Italy	164.18
1972	Klaus Dibiasi, Italy	504.12
1976	Klaus Dibiasi, Italy	600.51
1980	Falk Hoffmann, East Germany	835.65
1984	Greg Louganis, United States	710.91
1988	Greg Louganis, United States	638.61
1992	Sun Shuwei, China	677.31

WOMEN

SPRINGBOARD

		PTS
1920	Aileen Riggin, United States	539.90
1924	Elizabeth Becker, United States	474.50
1928	Helen Meany, United States	78.62
1932	Georgia Coleman, United States	87.52
1936	Marjorie Gestring, United States	89.27
1948	Victoria Draves, United States	108.74
1952	Patricia McCormick, United States	147.30
1956	Patricia McCormick, United States	142.36
1960	Ingrid Krämer, East Germany	155.81
1964	Ingrid Engel Krämer, East Germany	145.00
1968	Sue Gossick, United States	150.77
1972	Micki King, United States	450.03
1976	Jennifer Chandler, United States	506.19
1980	Irina Kalinina, USSR	725.91
1984	Sylvie Bernier, Canada	530.70
1988	Gao Min, China	580.23
1992	Gao Min, China	572.40

PLATFORM

		PTS
1912	Greta Johansson, Sweden	39.90
1920	Stefani Fryland-Clausen, Denmark	34.60
1924	Caroline Smith, United States	33.20
1928	Elizabeth B. Pinkston, United States	31.60
1932	Dorothy Poynton, United States	40.26
1936	Dorothy Poynton Hill, United States	33.93
1948	Victoria Draves, United States	68.87
1952	Patricia McCormick, United States	79.37
1956	Patricia McCormick, United States	84.85
1960	Ingrid Krämer, East Germany	91.28
1964	Lesley Bush, United States	99.80
1968	Milena Duchkova, Czechoslovakia	109.59
1972	Ulrika Knape, Sweden	390.00
1976	Elena Vaytsekhovskaya, USSR	406.59
1980	Martina Jäschke, East Germany	596.25
1984	Zhou Jihong, China	435.51
1988	Xu Yanmei, China	445.20
1992	Fu Mingxia, China	461.43

GYMNASTICS

MEN

ALL-AROUND

		PTS
1900	Gustave Sandras, France	302
1904	Julius Lenhart, Austria	69.80
1906	Pierre Paysse, France	97
1908	Alberto Braglia, Italy	317.0
1912	Alberto Braglia, Italy	135.0
1920	Giorgio Zampori, Italy	88.35
1924	Leon Stukelj, Yugoslavia	110.340
1928	Georges Miez, Switzerland	247.500
1932	Romeo Neri, Italy	140.625
1936	Alfred Schwarzmann, Germany	113.100
1948	Veikko Huhtanen, Finland	229.70
1952	Viktor Chukarin, USSR	115.70
1956	Viktor Chukarin, USSR	114.25
1960	Boris Shakhlin, USSR	115.95
1964	Yukio Endo, Japan	115.95
1968	Sawao Kato, Japan	115.90
1972	Sawao Kato, Japan	114.65
1976	Nikolai Andrianov, USSR	116.65
1980	Aleksandr Dityatin, USSR	118.65
1984	Koji Gushiken, Japan	118.70
1988	Vladimir Artemov, USSR	119.125
1992	Vitaly Scherbo, Unified Team	59.025

HORIZONTAL BAR

1896	Hermann Weingärtner, Germany	—
1900	Not held	
1904	Anton Heida, United States	40
1908-1920		Not held
1924	Leon Stukelj, Yugoslavia	19.73
1928	Georges Miez, Switzerland	19.17
1932	Dallas Bixler, United States	18.33
1936	Aleksanteri Saarvala, Finland	19.367
1948	Josef Stalder, Switzerland	19.85
1952	Jack Günthard, Switzerland	19.55
1956	Takashi Ono, Japan	19.60
1960	Takashi Ono, Japan	19.60
1964	Boris Shakhlin, USSR	19.625
1968	Akinori Nakayama, Japan	19.55
1972	Mitsuo Tsukahara, Japan	19.725
1976	Mitsuo Tsukahara, Japan	19.675
1980	Stoyan Deltchev, Bulgaria	19.825
1984	Shinji Morisue, Japan	20.00
1988	Vladimir Artemov, USSR	19.90
1992	Trent Dimas, United States	9.875

PARALLEL BARS

1896	Alfred Flatow, Germany	—
1900		Not held
1904	George Eyser, United States	44
1908-1920		Not held
1924	August Güttinger, Switzerland	21.63
1928	Ladislav Vacha, Czechoslovakia	18.83
1932	Romeo Neri, Italy	18.97
1936	Konrad Frey, Germany	19.067
1948	Michael Reusch, Switzerland	19.75

1952	Hans Eugster, Switzerland	19.65
1956	Viktor Chukarin, USSR	19.20
1960	Boris Shakhlin, USSR	19.40
1964	Yukio Endo, Japan	19.675
1968	Akinori Nakayama, Japan	19.475
1972	Sawao Kato, Japan	19.475
1976	Sawao Kato, Japan	19.675
1980	Aleksandr Tkachyov, USSR	19.775
1984	Bart Conner, United States	19.95
1988	Vladimir Artemov, USSR	19.925
1992	Vitaly Scherbo, Unified Team	9.900

LONG HORSE VAULT

1896	Karl Schumann, Germany	—
1900	Not held	
1904	George Eyser, United States	36
1908-1920		Not held
1924	Frank Kriz, United States	9.98
1928	Eugen Mack, Switzerland	9.58
1932	Savino Guglielmetti, Italy	18.03
1936	Alfred Schwarzmann, Germany	19.20
1948	Paavo Aaltonen, Finland	19.55
1952	Viktor Chukarin, USSR	19.20
1956	Helmut Bantz, Germany	18.85
1960	Takashi Ono, Japan	19.35
1964	Haruhiro Yamashita, Japan	19.60
1968	Mikhail Voronin, USSR	19.00
1972	Klaus Köste, East Germany	18.85
1976	Nikolai Andrianov, USSR	19.45
1980	Nikolai Andrianov, USSR	19.825
1984	Lou Yun, China	19.95
1988	Lou Yun, China	19.875
1992	Vitaly Scherbo, Unified Team	9.856

SIDE HORSE

1896	Louis Zutter, Switzerland	—
1900		Not held
1904	Anton Heida, United States	42
1908-1920		Not held
1924	Josef Wilhelm, Switzerland	21.23
1928	Hermann Hänggi, Switzerland	19.75
1932	Istvan Pelle, Hungary	19.07
1936	Konrad Frey, Germany	19.333
1948	Paavo Aaltonen, Finland	19.35
1952	Viktor Chukarin, USSR	19.50
1956	Boris Shakhlin, USSR	19.25
1960	Eugen Ekman, Finland	19.375
1964	Miroslav Cerar, Yugoslavia	19.525
1968	Miroslav Cerar, Yugoslavia	19.325
1972	Viktor Klimenko, USSR	19.125
1976	Zoltan Magyar, Hungary	19.70
1980	Zoltan Magyar, Hungary	19.925
1984	Li Ning, China	19.95
1988	Dmitri Bilozerchev, USSR	19.95
1992	Vitaly Scherbo, Unified Team	9.925

RINGS

1896	Ioannis Mitropoulos, Greece	—
1900	Not held	
1904	Hermann Glass, United States	45
1908-1920		Not held
1924	Francesco Martino, Italy	21.553
1928	Leon Stukelj, Yugoslavia	19.25
1932	George Gulack, United States	18.97
1936	Alois Hudec, Czechoslovakia	19.433
1948	Karl Frei, Switzerland	19.80
1952	Grant Shaginyan, USSR	19.75
1956	Albert Azaryan, USSR	19.35
1960	Albert Azaryan, USSR	19.725
1964	Takuji Haytta, Japan	19.475
1968	Akinori Nakayama, Japan	19.45
1972	Akinori Nakayama, Japan	19.35
1976	Nikolai Andrianov, USSR	19.65
1980	Aleksandr Dityatin, USSR	19.875
1984	Koji Gushiken, Japan	19.85
1988	Holger Behrendt, East Germany	19.925
1992	Vitaly Scherbo, Unified Team	9.937

FLOOR EXERCISES

1896-1928		Not held
1932	Istvan Pelle, Hungary	9.60
1936	Georges Miez, Switzerland	18.666
1948	Ferenc Pataki, Hungary	19.35
1952	K. William Thoresson, Sweden	19.25
1956	Valentin Muratov, USSR	19.20
1960	Nobuyuki Aihara, Japan	19.45
1964	Franco Menichelli, Italy	19.45
1968	Sawao Kato, Japan	19.475
1972	Nikolai Andrianov, USSR	19.175
1976	Nikolai Andrianov, USSR	19.45
1980	Roland Brückner, East Germany	19.75
1984	Li Ning, China	19.925
1988	Sergei Kharkov, USSR	19.925
1992	Li Xiaosahuang, China	9.925

TEAM COMBINED EXERCISES

1896-1900		Not held
1904	Turngemeinde Philadelphia	374.43
1906	Norway	19.00
1908	Sweden	438
1912	Italy	265.75
1920	Italy	359.855
1924	Italy	839.058
1928	Switzerland	1718.625
1932	Italy	541.850
1936	Germany	657.430
1948	Finland	1358.30
1952	USSR	574.40
1956	USSR	568.25
1960	Japan	575.20
1964	Japan	577.95
1968	Japan	575.90
1972	Japan	571.25
1976	Japan	576.85
1980	USSR	598.60
1984	United States	591.40
1988	USSR	593.35
1992	Unified Team	585.450

WOMEN

ALL-AROUND — PTS.

1952	Maria Gorokhovskaya, USSR	76.78
1956	Larissa Latynina, USSR	74.933
1960	Larissa Latynina, USSR	77.031
1964	Vera Caslavska, Czechoslovakia	77.564
1968	Vera Caslavska, Czechoslovakia	78.25
1972	Lyudmila Tousischeva, USSR	77.025
1976	Nadia Comaneci, Romania	79.275
1980	Yelena Davydova, USSR	79.15
1984	Mary Lou Retton, United States	79.175
1988	Yelena Shushunova, USSR	79.662
1992	Tatiana Gutsu, Unified Team	39.737

SIDE HORSE VAULT

1952	Yekaterina Kalinchuk, USSR	19.20
1956	Larissa Latynina, USSR	18.833
1960	Margarita Nikolayeva, USSR	19.316
1964	Vera Caslavska, Czechoslovakia	19.483
1968	Vera Caslavska, Czechoslovakia	19.775
1972	Karin Janz, East Germany	19.525
1976	Nelli Kim, USSR	19.80
1980	Natalya Shaposhnikova, USSR	19.725
1984	Ecaterina Szabo, Romania	19.875
1988	Svetlana Boginskaya, USSR	19.905
1992	Henrietta Onodi, Hungary	9.925
	Lavinia Milosovici, Romania	9.925

UNEVEN BARS

1952	Margit Korondi, Hungary	19.40
1956	Agnes Keleti, Hungary	18.966
1960	Polina Astakhova, USSR	19.616
1964	Polina Astakhova, USSR	19.332

1968	Vera Caslavska, Czechoslovakia	19.65
1972	Karin Janz, East Germany	19.675
1976	Nadia Comaneci, Romania	20.00
1980	Maxi Gnauck, East Germany	19.875
1984	Ma Yanhong, China	19.95
1988	Daniela Silivas, Romania	20.00
1992	Lu Li, China	10.00

BALANCE BEAM
1952	Nina Bocharova, USSR	19.22
1956	Agnes Keleti, Hungary	18.80
1960	Eva Bosakova, Czechoslovakia	19.283
1964	Vera Caslavska, Czechoslovakia	19.449
1968	Natalya Kuchinskaya, USSR	19.65
1972	Olga Korbut, USSR	19.40
1976	Nadia Comaneci, Romania	19.95
1980	Nadia Comaneci, Romania	19.80
1984	Simona Pauca, Romania	19.80
1988	Daniela Silivas, Romania	19.924
1992	Tatiana Lisenko, Unified Team	9.975

FLOOR EXERCISES
1952	Agnes Keleti, Hungary	19.36
1956	Agnes Keleti, Hungary	18.733
1960	Larissa Latynina, USSR	19.583
1964	Larissa Latynina, USSR	19.599
1968	Vera Caslavska, Czechoslovakia	19.675
1972	Olga Korbut, USSR	19.575
1976	Nelli Kim, USSR	19.85
1980	Nadia Comaneci, Romania	19.875
1984	Ecaterina Szabo, Romania	19.975
1988	Daniela Silivas, Romania	19.937
1992	Lavinia Milosovici, Romania	10.00

TEAM COMBINED EXERCISES
1928	Holland	316.75
1932	Not held	
1936	Germany	506.50
1948	Czechoslovakia	445.45
1952	USSR	527.03
1956	USSR	444.800
1960	USSR	382.320
1964	USSR	280.890
1968	USSR	382.85
1972	USSR	380.50
1976	USSR	466.00
1980	USSR	394.90
1984	Romania	392.02
1988	USSR	395.475
1992	Unified Team	395.666

RHYTHMIC ALL-AROUND
1984	Lori Fung, Canada	57.95
1988	Marina Lobach, USSR	60.00
1992	Aleksandra Timoshenko, Unified Team	59.037

WINTER GAMES

BOBSLED

4-MAN BOB
1924	Switzerland (Eduard Scherrer)	5:45.54
1928	United States (William Fiske) (5-man)	3:20.50
1932	United States (William Fiske)	7:53.68
1936	Switzerland (Pierre Musy)	5:19.85
1948	United States (Francis Tyler)	5:20.10
1952	Germany (Andreas Ostler)	5:07.84
1956	Switzerland (Franz Kapus)	5:10.44
1960	Not held	
1964	Canada (Victor Emery)	4:14.46
1968	Italy (Eugenio Monti) (2 runs)	2:17.39
1972	Switzerland (Jean Wicki)	4:43.07
1976	East Germany (Meinhard Nehmer)	3:40.43

1980	East Germany (Meinhard Nehmer)	3:59.92
1984	East Germany (Wolfgang Hoppe)	3:20.22
1988	Switzerland (Ekkehard Fasser)	3:47.51
1992	Austria (Ingo Appelt)	3:53.90

Note: Driver in parentheses.

2-MAN BOB
1932	United States (Hubert Stevens)	8:14.74
1936	United States (Ivan Brown)	5:29.29
1948	Switzerland (Felix Endrich)	5:29.20
1952	Germany (Andreas Ostler)	5:24.54
1956	Italy (Lamberto Dalla Costa)	5:30.14
1960	Not held	
1964	Great Britain (Anthony Nash)	4:21.90
1968	Italy (Eugenio Monti)	4:41.54
1972	West Germany (Wolfgang Zimmerer)	4:57.07
1976	East Germany (Meinhard Nehmer)	3:44.42
1980	Switzerland (Erich Schärer)	4:09.36
1984	East Germany (Wolfgang Hoppe)	3:25.56
1988	USSR (Janis Kipours)	3:53.48
1992	Switzerland (Gustav Weder)	4:03.26

Note: Driver in parentheses.

ICE HOCKEY
1920*	Canada, United States, Czechoslovakia
1924	Canada, United States, Great Britain
1928	Canada, Sweden, Switzerland
1932	Canada, United States, Germany
1936	Great Britain, Canada, United States
1948	Canada, Czechoslovakia, Switzerland
1952	Canada, United States, Sweden
1956	USSR, United States, Canada
1960	United States, Canada, USSR
1964	USSR, Sweden, Czechoslovakia
1968	USSR, Czechoslovakia, Canada
1972	USSR, United States, Czechoslovakia
1976	USSR, Czechoslovakia, West Germany
1980	United States, USSR, Sweden
1984	USSR, Czechoslovakia, Sweden
1988	USSR, Finland, Sweden
1992	Unified Team, Canada, Czechoslovakia

*Competition held at summer games in Antwerp.

Note: Gold, silver, and bronze medals.

FIGURE SKATING

MEN

SINGLES
1908*	Ulrich Salchow, Sweden
1920#	Gillis Grafström, Sweden
1924	Gillis Grafström, Sweden
1928	Gillis Grafström, Sweden
1932	Karl Schäfer, Austria
1936	Karl Schäfer, Austria
1948	Dick Button, United States
1952	Dick Button, United States
1956	Hayes Alan Jenkins, United States
1960	David Jenkins, United States
1964	Manfred Schnelldorfer, West Germany
1968	Wolfgang Schwarz, Austria
1972	Ondrej Nepela, Czechoslovakia
1976	John Curry, Great Britain
1980	Robin Cousins, Great Britain
1984	Scott Hamilton, United States
1988	Brian Boitano, United States
1992	Viktor Petrenko, Unified Team

WOMEN

SINGLES
1908*	Madge Syers, Great Britain
1920#	Magda Julin, Sweden

PHOTOGRAPHY CREDITS

FRONT COVER
Neil Leifer

BACK COVER
Manny Millan

FRONT MATTER
2-3, Stefan Warter

INTRODUCTION
6, The Metropolitan Museum of Art, Rogers Fund, 1914; 8, The Metropolitan Museum of Art, Rogers Fund, 1905

THE GAMES ARE REBORN
10-11, Cumberland County Historical Society; 12, International Olympic Committee; 14, Missouri Historical Society; 15, International Olympic Committee; 16, Missouri Historical Society; 17, International Olympic Committee; 18 top, United States Olympic Committee, bottom, Brown Brothers; 19, International Olympic Committee; 20-21, Roger-Viollet; 21, Brown Brothers; 22, top Missouri Historical Society, bottom Missouri Historical Society; 23, Brown Brothers; 24, top UPI/Bettmann Newsphotos, bottom International Olympic Committee; 25, International Olympic Committee; 26, top Culver Pictures, bottom International Olympic Committee; 27, Brown Brothers; 28, International Olympic Committee; 29, UPI/Bettmann Newsphotos; 30, Roger-Viollet; 31, Amateur Athletic Foundation of Los Angeles;

THE GAMES GROW UP
32-33, FPG International; 34, Ullstein Bilderdienst; 36, FPG International; 37, Ullstein Bilderdienst; 38, UPI/Bettmann Newsphotos; 39, UPI/Bettmann Newsphotos; 40-41, UPI/Bettmann Newsphotos; 42, UPI/Bettmann Newsphotos; 43, top UPI/Bettmann Newsphotos, bottom United States Olympic Committee; 44, UPI/Bettmann Newsphotos; 45, Nicolas Muray/ International Museum of Photography at George Eastman House; 46-47, UPI/Bettmann Newsphotos; 48 top UPI/Bettmann Newsphotos; 49, Illustration/Sygma; 50, UPI/Bettmann Newsphotos; 51, Ullstein Bilderdienst; 52, Ullstein Bilderdienst; 53 top International Olympic Committee, bottom United States Olympic Committee; 54-55, UPI/Bettmann Newsphotos;

56, UPI/Bettmann Newsphotos; 57, Delmar Watson Los Angeles Archives; 58-59, Delmar Watson Los Angeles Archives; 59, top UPI/Bettmann Newsphotos, bottom Security National Bank Collection, Los Angeles Public Library; 60-61, top FPG International; 60, bottom UPI/Bettmann Newsphotos; 61, bottom Illustration/Sygma; 62, International Olympic Committee; 63, Süddeutscher Verlag; 64-65, Ullstein Bilderdienst; 66-67, FPG International; 67, UPI/Bettmann Newsphotos; 68, Culver Pictures 69, United States Olympic Committee; 70, United States Olympic Committee; 71, International Olympic Committee; 72, International Olympic Committee; 73, UPI/Bettmann Newsphotos;

THE GAMES EXPAND
74-75, George Silk/LIFE; 76, UPI/Bettmann Newsphotos; 78, International Olympic Committee; 79, AP/Wide World; 80, Edward Clark/LIFE; 81, The Durant Collection; 82, top International Olympic Committee, bottom FPG International; 83, FPG International; 84, Mark Kauffman/ LIFE; 85, Mark Kauffman/LIFE; 86, Ralph Crane/LIFE; 87; N. R. Farbman/ LIFE; 88, Mark Kauffman/LIFE; 89, Ralph Crane/ LIFE; 90, top Ullstein Bilderdienst, bottom UPI/Bettmann Newsphotos; 91, UPI/Bettmann Newsphotos; 92, John Dominis/LIFE; 93, Richard Meek; 94, top Richard Meek, bottom John G. Zimmerman; 95, John Dominis/LIFE; 96, AP/Wide World; 97, James Whitmore/ LIFE; 98, Archive Photos; 99, UPI/ Bettmann Newsphotos; 100, top AP/Wide World; 100-101, John G. Zimmerman; 102, top AP/Wide World, bottom George Silk/LIFE; 103, Jerry Cooke; 104, AP/Wide World; 105, UPI/Bettmann Newsphotos; 106, Presse Sports; 107, Jerry Cooke; 108, AP/Wide World; 109, Ullstein Bilderdienst; 110, International Olympic Committee; 111, Mark Kauffman/LIFE;

THE GAMES GO GLOBAL
112-113, Heinz Kluetmeier; 114, George Silk/LIFE; 116, United States Olympic Committee; 117, Neil Leifer; 118, Arthur Rickerby/LIFE; 119, Takeo Tanuma; 120-121, top Richard Meek, bottom Jerry Cooke; 121, George Silk/LIFE; 122, Ralph Crane/LIFE; 123, top Jerry Cooke, bottom Ralph Crane/LIFE; 124, Neil

Leifer; 125, Ken Regan/Camera 5; 126, top Neil Leifer, bottom Jerry Cooke; 127, Tony Duffy/ ALLSPORT U.S.A.; 128, John G. Zimmerman; 129, John G. Zimmerman; 130, James Drake; 131, Neil Leifer; 132, Jerry Cooke; 133, top Jerry Cooke, bottom Rich Clarkson; 134-135, Takeo Tanuma; 136, Heinz Kluetmeier; 137, Neil Leifer; 138, Neil Leifer; 139, Tony Triolo; 140, Helmut Gritscher; 141, Helmut Gritscher; 142, Neil Leifer; 143, John G. Zimmerman/LIFE; 144, Jerry Cooke; 145, Caryn Levy; 146, William Campbell; 147, Co Rentmeester/ LIFE; 148, Jerry Cooke; 149, Walter Iooss, Jr.; 150, Curt Gunther/Camera 5.; 151, Heinz Kluetmeier; 152, Jerry Cooke; 153, Neil Leifer; 154, Tony Duffy; 155, Neil Leifer;

THE COMMERCIAL GAMES
156-157, Heinz Kluetmeier; 158, Jerry Cooke; 160, Heinz Kluetmeier; 161, Ronald C. Modra; 162, Heinz Kluetmeier; 163, Rich Clarkson; 164-165, Heinz Kluetmeier; 166, top Eric Schweikardt, bottom George Tiedemann; 167, Heinz Kluetmeier; 168, Bob Langer/Chicago Tribune Company; 169, Neil Leifer; 170, top Andy Hayt, bottom John W. McDonough; 170-171, Neil Leifer; 172, Tony Tomsic; 173, Tony Tomsic; 174, Ronald C. Modra; 175, Heinz Kluetmeier; 176-177, Ronald C. Modra; 177, top John W. McDonough, bottom Mike Powell/ALLSPORT U.S.A.; 178, top Bill Eppridge, bottom Richard Mackson; 179, Carl Yarbrough; 180, Richard Mackson; 181, John Biever; 182-183, Bill Frakes; 183, John W. McDonough; 184-185, Ronald C. Modra; 186, Heinz Kluetmeier; 187, Peter Read Miller; 188, Heinz Kluetmeier; 189, Rich Clarkson; 190, Bob Martin/ALLSPORT U.S.A. 191, Theo Westenberger; 192, Walter Iooss, Jr./©1984 Fuji Film, U.S.A., Inc.; 193, Yann Guichaoula/ VANDYSTADT/ALLSPORT U.S.A.; 194, Walter Iooss, Jr./©1984 Fuji Film, U.S.A., Inc.; 195, Heinz Kluetmeier; 196, Tony Duffy/ALLSPORT U.S.A.; 197, VANDYSTADT/ALLSPORT U.S.A.; 198, Richard Martin/VANDYSTADT/ ALLSPORT U.S.A.; 199, Klaus Titzer/ GAMMA LIAISON;

THE FUTURE
200, Peter Read Miller; 202, John G. Zimmerman.

INDEX